Japan and China
A Contest in Aid to Sub-Saharan Africa

Japan and China
A Contest in Aid to Sub-Saharan Africa

Koichi Sakamoto
Toyo University, Japan

NEW JERSEY · LONDON · SINGAPORE · BEIJING · SHANGHAI · HONG KONG · TAIPEI · CHENNAI · TOKYO

Published by

World Scientific Publishing Co. Pte. Ltd.
5 Toh Tuck Link, Singapore 596224
USA office: 27 Warren Street, Suite 401-402, Hackensack, NJ 07601
UK office: 57 Shelton Street, Covent Garden, London WC2H 9HE

Library of Congress Cataloging-in-Publication Data
Names: Sakamoto, Koichi, 1953– author.
Title: Japan and China : a contest in aid to Sub-Saharan Africa / Koichi Sakamoto.
Description: Hackensack, New Jersey : World Scientific, 2018. |
    Includes bibliographical references and index.
Identifiers: LCCN 2017049101 | ISBN 9789813223738 (hardcover)
Subjects: LCSH: Economic assistance, Japanese--Africa, Sub-Saharan. | Economic assistance,
    Chinese--Africa, Sub-Saharan. | Africa, Sub-Saharan--Economic conditions. |
    Africa, Sub-Saharan--Foreign economic relations--Japan. | Africa, Sub-Saharan--
    Foreign economic relations--China. | Japan--Foreign economic relations--Africa,
    Sub-Saharan. | China--Foreign economic relations--Africa, Sub-Saharan.
Classification: LCC HC800 .S238 2018 | DDC 338.91506--dc23
LC record available at https://lccn.loc.gov/2017049101

British Library Cataloguing-in-Publication Data
A catalogue record for this book is available from the British Library.

Copyright © 2018 by World Scientific Publishing Co. Pte. Ltd.

All rights reserved. This book, or parts thereof, may not be reproduced in any form or by any means, electronic or mechanical, including photocopying, recording or any information storage and retrieval system now known or to be invented, without written permission from the publisher.

For photocopying of material in this volume, please pay a copying fee through the Copyright Clearance Center, Inc., 222 Rosewood Drive, Danvers, MA 01923, USA. In this case permission to photocopy is not required from the publisher.

For any available supplementary material, please visit
http://www.worldscientific.com/worldscibooks/10.1142/10539#t=suppl

Desk Editor: Jiang Yulin

Typeset by Stallion Press
Email: enquiries@stallionpress.com

Printed in Singapore

Contents

List of Tables ix

Introduction xi

Chapter 1   Aid to Africa by Western Countries   1

1.1   Introduction of Conditional Aid in the Early 1980s   1
    1.1.1   Aid Dependence and the "Washington Consensus"   1
    1.1.2   Revolutionary Aid Reforms   7
1.2   From Aid to Private Investment in the 21st Century   10
    1.2.1   Africa's Buoyant Economy after Debt Cancellation   10
    1.2.2   Failure of a New Aid Regime?   12

Chapter 2   Aid to Sub-Saharan Africa by Japan   17

2.1   From Asian Donor to Western Donor   17
    2.1.1   Toward Becoming the No.1 Donor for 10 Years   18
    2.1.2   Opposition to the "Washington Consensus" in Africa   34
2.2   Path to Global Donor   38
    2.2.1   Tackling Global Issues with the U.S.   38
    2.2.2   From Defeat in the Gulf War to Initiatives for Fragile States   40
2.3   Implications for China's Aid   44

Chapter 3	Aid to Sub-Saharan Africa by China	47
3.1	From Tazara Railway to Major Economic Partner	47
	3.1.1 Surge of Economic Powers since the 1980s	48
	3.1.2 Commitment to South–South Cooperation	70
3.2	Champion as an Emerging Donor	75
	3.2.1 China's Overwhelming Presence in Africa	75
	3.2.2 From "Washington Consensus" to "Beijing Consensus"	79
3.3	Achievements and Trends	86

Chapter 4	Rivalry between Japan and China until Early 2010s	89
4.1	Japan's Conservative Regime and Reaction from China	89
	4.1.1 Conservative Party and China	89
	4.1.2 Opposition Party and China	95
4.2	Tokyo International Conference on African Development (TICAD) vs. Forum on China-Africa Cooperation (FOCAC)	96
	4.2.1 TICAD since 1993 and Achievements	96
	4.2.2 FOCAC since 2000 and Achievements	97
4.3	Collaboration between Two Countries	98
	4.3.1 Collaboration with Other Countries	98
	4.3.2 Japan's Collaboration with China	99

Chapter 5	Contest between Japan and China from 2012 to 2020s	101
5.1	Rival Administrations of Japan and China	101
	5.1.1 Abe Administration	101
	5.1.2 Xi Administration	105
	5.1.3 Close Competition in Aid to Africa	106
5.2	Future Policy Directions	110
	5.2.1 Possibilities of Collaboration between the Two Countries	110
	5.2.2 Contest Further?	113

Chapter 6	**Case Studies**	**115**
6.1	Djibouti: Japanese Army versus Chinese Army	115
6.2	Kenya: Top Recipient of Japan's ODA versus Maritime Silk Road from China	118
6.3	Malawi: Japan's Grassroots Support versus Nation Building by China	120

Chapter 7	**Concluding Remarks**	**125**

References 129

Index 133

List of Tables

Introduction   xi

A Gross Concessional Financing for Development
("ODA-like" Flows), 2013   xiv

Chapter 1   Aid to Africa by Western Countries   1

1-1   IMF Lending Arrangements as of February 28, 2017   4
1-2   Foreign Investment in Major African and Asian Countries   11

Chapter 2   Aid to Sub-Saharan Africa by Japan   17

2-1   Macro-Economic Performance of Japan and China   19
2-2   Principal Trade Partners of Africa   21
2-3   Foreign Direct Investment (FDI) by Japan and China   21
2-4   Japan's Relationships with Africa   22
2-5   Economic Cooperation by Major Donors (Million US$)   25
2-6   Foreign Aid by Japan and China   27
2-7   Top Recipients of Japan's ODA   30
2-8   Development Banks   31
2-9   Japan's ODA Charter 1992   35
2-10   Development Cooperation Charter 2015   41

Chapter 3   Aid to Sub-Saharan Africa by China   47

3-1   China's Relationships with Africa   52
3-2   Estimates of Concessional Finance for Development
(ODA-like Flows) of Key Providers of Development   59

3-3 Agreement of Loans Concluded with China
    EXIM 2011–2013 (Côte d'Ivoire)   62
3-4 Eight Principles for Economic Aid and Technical
    Assistance to Other Countries (1964)   73
3-5 Basic Features of China's Foreign Aid Policy in
    the White Paper 2011   82

Chapter 4   Rivalry between Japan and China until Early 2010s   89

4-1 History of Administrations   90

Chapter 6   Case Studies   115

6-1 China's Investment in Djibouti (2016)   116
6-2 Debt Sustainability of Djibouti   117
6-3 Malawi: Public and Publicly-Guaranteed External Debt   122

Introduction

In December 2015, at a conference hall in Johannesburg, South Africa, Xi Jinping, President of China, was in front of heads of state and top officials from 50 countries of the African continent. The African leaders were invited to attend a summit meeting of the Forum on China-Africa Cooperation (FOCAC), which has been held at the ministerial level every three years since 2000. Xi surprised the audience and the media by pledging 60 billion U.S. dollars in the coming three years.

Eight months later, in August 2016, Shinzo Abe, the Prime Minister of Japan, was in Nairobi, Kenya, to attend a summit meeting of the Tokyo International Conference on African Development (TICAD). Addressing the heads of state and top officials of the 50 African states, he pledged 30 billion U.S. dollars over three years. The amount seemed smaller than that of China, but he had also pledged 32 billion U.S. dollars at the last TICAD in Yokohama, Japan, in 2013.

The latest Japanese meeting, to which the heads of state have been invited since 1993, was the first such gathering in three years. This three-year interval is the same as that for FOCAC. In addition, this meeting was held for the first time in Africa. FOCAC had been alternatively held in China and Africa since its first meeting in 2000.

The two leaders were rivals within the context of a chilly relationship between Japan and China. Xi was elected General Secretary of the Communist Party in November 2012. Abe was elected Prime Minister in December of the same year. Their elections came soon after the serious rioting in 50 cities in China, where rioters were protesting the nationalization of disputed islands by the government of Japan in September.

Overtaking Japan in economic size in 2010, China became the second-largest economy after the U.S. and is currently a major emerging donor for African development. Japan, as a member of the Group of 7 (G7) and of the Development Assistance Committee (DAC) of the Organization for Economic Co-operation and Development (OECD), has had a long history of aid to Africa, too. These two Asian economic giants have been competing on many fronts, including political and economic ones, in recent years. As both leaders may stay in power until the early 2020s, it is important to understand their contest in aid to Africa.

China's overwhelming presence in Africa has been a hot issue when one thinks about economic development in the continent and relationships with donors. There has been much coverage in newspapers, magazines, reports and analyses on China's massive intervention in African economic and political affairs. Special attention is paid to China's activities because its intervention, especially with regard to aid to Africa, has been different from that of Western countries.

This intervention has looked like a threat even to experts at the OECD and the Agence Française de Développement (AFD, French Development Agency) whom I met in Paris from 2010. Paying attention to the differences in China's aid, they showed their strong disapproval of the massive Chinese investment in Africa outside the aid system, which had been designed with enormous efforts for reform by Western donors.

On the contrary, Chinese scholars and researchers whom I met in Beijing, Tianjin, and Shanghai every year from 2008 onward were proud of their march to Africa during the period. However, they were curious about Western criticism regarding their endeavors to develop Africa. By the time during my visit to China in May 2017, they had become confident about their contribution to African development and the international community. It is also true that the Chinese had taken into account international standards and codes for foreign aid by that point.

Japan has tried to be a "Western" donor with the passive (to some extent) assimilation of aid reforms led by European countries after the end of the Cold War in the early 1990s. China, as a follower of Japan's development approach, paid attention to Japan's policies for aid to developing countries, including African ones.

In this context, the objective of this publication is to conduct a brief survey of aid to Sub-Saharan Africa (SSA) by Japan and China and make some projections until the early 2020s about how such aid will develop. The independent analyses will be followed by comparisons of aid to Sub-Saharan Africa by the two Asian giants. Analytical methods include a literature survey and some data analyses. Thorough reviews of statements by both governments are made. Some analyses are conducted on the overall economic development in the two countries (e.g., the surge of China's economic power and Japan's Abenomics), their aid policies, and aid reforms by DAC countries.

In addition to a literature survey, basic empirical analyses are conducted based on statistics on their aid and economies. Aid is analyzed in the context of overall economic cooperation composed of official aid and private investment. The analyses on China are supplemented by the author's interviews with Chinese scholars and experts as well as Western experts of the OECD and the AFD. Short surveys of some African countries will be presented, but a cross-country analysis occupies the central part of this book.

Regarding the subjects of this publication, it will deal with their aid to SSA. Though TICAD and FOCAC are aid systems for all African countries, including countries in North Africa, this book focuses on SSA. There are a few differences among the organizations concerned about the definition of SSA. Following classifications by the World Bank and the International Monetary Fund (IMF), Sudan, South Sudan, and Mauritania are included in the definition of SSA in this book. This is important because there are substantial investments in Sudan and South Sudan by the Chinese.

Regarding aid or foreign aid, the author pays attention to official aid, which is aid provided by official organizations. The OECD/DAC provides definitions of aid. Japan is a member of the DAC, while China is not. It is unknown whether China uses the same definitions of aid in its publications, including statistical yearbooks. In the publications of OECD/DAC, economic cooperation is composed of official development assistance (ODA), official other flows (OOF), private funds, and non-profit funds by nongovernmental organizations (NGOs). These funding lines are referred to as *resources to developing countries* in the publications of OECD and of the government of Japan. The author tries to use data on China's aid under this ODA definition and composition.

ODA is defined as loans with more than a 25 percent grant element. We are not sure of this requirement in China's data on aid. There are some analyses of data on loans from China to recipient countries. It is also difficult to obtain terms of financing by China's official banks, especially The Export–Import Bank of China (China EXIM). The activities of China EXIM may be included not only in ODA but also in OOF. Following OECD/DAC documents, this book uses terms like "*ODA-like*" and "*OOF-like*" for China. It should be noted that China EXIM has provided

Table A   Gross Concessional Financing for Development ("ODA-like" Flows), 2013

Country	USD Bn (Updated December 19, 2014; Updated Country Estimates on September 29, 2014)	Gross ODA/GNI
United States	31.77	0.19%
Japan	22.53	0.44%
United Kingdom	18.34	0.74%
Germany	16.22	0.43%
France	12.88	0.46%
Sweden	5.89	1.03%
Saudi Arabia	5.83	0.78%
Norway	5.67	1.09%
Netherlands	5.61	0.70%
United Arab Emirates	5.49	1.43%
Canada	4.99	0.28%
Australia	4.92	0.32%
Italy	3.49	0.17%
Turkey	3.31	0.41%
Switzerland	3.22	0.47%
Denmark	3.10	0.90%
China (People's Rep.)	3.01	0.03%
Spain	2.60	0.19%
Belgium	2.36	0.46%
South Korea	1.82	0.14%

Source: OECD, *Development Co-operation Report 2015*.

substantial amounts of loans to SSA. Table A shows a latest picture of ODA and "ODA-like" by major donors. China's figure captures only bilateral aid and excludes enormous amounts of loans by China EXIM.

This book is recommended for those interested in understanding East Asian international relations, contemporary aid trends, and issues in Sub-Saharan Africa. This publication was realized with the strong support of World Scientific. I express my sincere thanks to them. Special thanks go to Mr. Jiang Yulin, editor of the Singaporean branch of World Scientific. In fact, the preparation of this publication was initiated by him after he read my comments in AFP press on TICAD in August 2016 after FOCAC in December 2015. His wise guidance during the preparation of the manuscript and accurate advice together with his kindness and patience are highly appreciated. The author is responsible for all remaining errors and mistakes.

Koichi SAKAMOTO
May 2017

Chapter 1

Aid to Africa by Western Countries

In this chapter, a short history of aid to Africa by Western countries and the current aid regime for the continent will be analyzed. This serves as a basis to understand trends and policies of aid by Japan and China and their competition to provide aid to Sub-Saharan Africa.

Facing a financial crisis in the late 1970s, many African countries were forced to take a market-oriented approach to aid receipt (called the "Washington Consensus"). In the framework of structural adjustment, a new aid regime was introduced by Western donors. Though this regime is embodied in the current world, there have been new dimensions to development in the 21st century. Thus, the author focuses on the past achievements and current policies and the aid for Africa in this context to understand aid by Japan and China in the subsequent chapters.

Section 1.1 will analyze how the approach became a condition to aid, its concomitant aid reforms, and the poor results for African development. Section 1.2 will look at the shift from aid to private flows after debt cancellations by Western donors, including Japan.

1.1 Introduction of Conditional Aid in the Early 1980s

1.1.1 *Aid Dependence and the "Washington Consensus"*

After independence from colonial rule, many African countries followed import substitution strategies led by their governments in the same way as those in other developing countries. Though some progress was made in their development, the competitiveness of their economies deteriorated. As their income levels were low and their political situations were not favorable to foreign investment, the countries continued to depend on foreign aid to develop their economies.

With the high prices of commodities caused by two oil shocks during the 1970s, the countries borrowed substantial amounts of money to finance their development, especially infrastructure. In the late 1970s, however, commodity prices fell significantly and, coupled with high interest rates in the U.S., many African countries faced serious debt crises. To cope with the crises, they resorted to the IMF and the World Bank for assistance. These institutions are often called the Bretton Woods Institutions (BWIs) because they had been created just after the end of World War II in Bretton Woods, New Hampshire. Their objective was to assist member countries in reconstructing their economies and their economic development after the war. In return for aid and loans to relieve their debts, the African countries were forced to take a market-oriented approach in their economic framework, called the Structural Adjustment Program (SAP), set by the BWIs.

This market-oriented approach was initiated by the Thatcher administration in the U.K. and the Reagan administration in the U.S.[1] They put pressure on developed countries like Japan during bilateral economic talks, and used the BWIs to request that developing countries take liberal measures, too. The approach was called the "Washington Consensus," a consensus among Wall Street investors, the U.S. Treasury, and the BWIs.[2] This approach was imposed on developing countries including African economies, most of which were low income. The implementation of the

---

[1] There were many reports like the following article by Rachman, G., from the U.K. Financial Times on December 15, 2009: "The closing of the Thatcher era," in which the experiment with Thatcherism since the early 1980s led to the global financial crisis starting in 2008.

[2] The word, "Washington Consensus" was invented by John Williamson of the U.S. Peterson Institute for International Economics in his article in 1989. Its summary was presented in the following article: Williamson, J., "From Reform Agenda: A Short History of the Washington Consensus and Suggestions for What to Do Next," *Finance & Development*, September 2003, pp. 10–11. https://people.ucsc.edu/~hutch/Econ143/historywash.pdf (May 13, 2017).

liberal policies became a condition to aid. This paradigm started in the early 1980s and continues until today.

Table 1-1 shows the latest loans by the IMF to low-income countries including many African countries.

There are many African countries that have arrangements with the IMF. Kenya, which started SAP in 1980 for the first time, is still under IMF's control.

In more detail, structural adjustment started in 1980 when the World Bank provided Structural Adjustment Loans (SALs) to developing countries. The Philippines, Kenya, Senegal, and Sudan were the first borrowers. The IMF, which had given short-term loans, started the Structural Adjustment Facility (SAF) in 1986 and the Enhanced Structural Adjustment Facility (ESAF) in 1987. These facilities were introduced so that the IMF could cope with the medium-term structural adjustment of recipient countries. Many African countries, together with other developing countries, especially in Latin America, had to adopt SAPs forced by the BWIs.

The background to the beginning of SAP was that the World Bank and bilateral donors realized that aid given to African countries was not meeting its objectives. In 1981, the World Bank published a report on African development and aid[3] after making a thorough review of the achievements of SSA since the end of World War II. The SAP mechanism was proposed. Its objective was to make recipient countries go from dependency on aid to a model based on private investment.[4] The author's more concrete explanation of this is that recipient countries should have an economic system to repay external debt and to sustain their growth and development through private investment. Creditworthiness should be established so that they can resort to investment by private enterprises and not official aid. Private investment included foreign investment. That is why liberalization of capital markets, or encouragement of foreign direct investment (FDI) and portfolio investment, was introduced in SAPs.

---

[3] World Bank, *Accelerated Development in Sub-Saharan Africa: An Agenda for Action*, 1981. http://documents.worldbank.org/curated/en/702471468768312009/pdf/multi-page.pdf

[4] The objective is related to a series of liberal measures. Both the objectives and measures are published as IMF policy intentions documents like letters of intent for many countries.

Table 1-1 IMF Lending Arrangements as of February 28, 2017

			(In Thousands of SDRs)		
Member	Date of Arrangement	Expiration	Total Amount Agreed	Undrawn Balance	IMF Credit Outstanding under PRGFT
Poverty Reduction and Growth Trust (PRGT)					
Extended Credit Facility (ECF)					
Afghanistan	20-Jul-16	19-Jul-19	32,380	27,880	45,450
Burkina Faso	27-Dec-13	26-Sep-17	55,640	4,470	153,805
Central African Republic	20-Jul-16	19-Jul-19	83,550	58,500	80,797
Chad	01-Aug-14	30-Nov-17	140,200	41,860	89,847
Cote d'Ivoire	12-Dec-16	11-Dec-19	162,600	139,371	742,897
Ghana	03-Apr-15	02-Apr-18	664,200	332,100	655,317
Grenada	26-Jun-14	25-Jun-17	14,040	2,000	21,229
Guinea-Bissau	10-Jul-15	09-Jul-18	17,040	9,088	18,020
Kyrgyz Republic	08-Apr-15	07-Apr-18	66,600	28,544	139,876
Liberia	19-Nov-12	18-Nov-17	111,664	14,764	143,398
Madagascar	27-Jul-16	26-Nov-19	220,000	188,572	102,152
Malawi	23-Jul-12	30-Jun-17	138,800	19,500	150,409
Mali	18-Dec-13	17-Dec-17	98,000	38,000	124,265
Moldova, Republic of	07-Nov-16	06-Nov-19	43,100	34,400	154,615
Niger	23-Jan-17	22-Jan-20	98,700	84,600	128,331
Sao Tome & Principe	13-Jul-15	12-Jul-18	4,440	2,537	3,673
Total			1,950,954	1,026,186	2,754,080
Standby Credit Facility (SCF)					
Kenya	14-Mar-16	13-Mar-18	354,629	354,629	550,250
Mozambique	18-Dec-15	17-Jun-17	204,480	119,280	146,424
Rwanda	08-Jun-16	07-Dec-17	144,180	36,045	109,974
Total			703,289	509,954	806,648

Source: International Monetary Fund (IMF).

Based on the relevant documents,[5] the author summarizes the general characteristics of the measures to achieve this objective as follows:

— Country Approach (Macro Approach)
The past approach was a project approach. Individual donors provided their own projects. There was no overall framework for development and project aid. Taking the macro approach, requirements of investment (projects) for development and donor support are forecast in consistency with the actual economic situations.

— Aid Coordination
In relation to the previous characteristic, there was no coordination of projects by individual donors in the past. It was felt that introducing aid coordination could help to avoid the duplication of projects, dependence on aid, and difficulties in debt repayment. Donor coordination meetings were introduced for the overall economy, and each of the major sectors was to plan appropriate projects.

— Conditionalities Included the Liberalizations of Markets
Debt relief, aid, and loans can be given with the condition that the countries concerned take market-oriented policies. The policy measures proposed by the IMF and the World Bank were called "conditionalities." They covered the macroeconomy, sectors, projects, and government and public enterprises. The author could summarize the major policy groups as follows: the opening of domestic markets like import and investment liberalization, liberalization of domestic markets including factor markets,

---

[5] Mosley, P. et al., *Aid and Power: The World Bank and Policy-Based Lending Volume 1*, Routledge, 1991. There is "An appendix to Chapter 2: A Sample Policy-Based Lending Agreement (dated February 1987)" on pages 56–61. Toye, J., "Structural Adjustment: Context, Assumptions, Origin and Diversity," Van der Hoeven, R., & Van der Kraaij, F. (eds) *Structual Adjustment and Beyond in Sub-Saharan Africa*, Ministry of Foreign Affairs, the Hague, 1994. Killick, T., *IMF Programmes in Developing Countries: Design and Impact*, Routledge for Overseas Development Institute, 1995. IMF, "Theoretical Aspects of the Design of Fund-Supported Adjustment Program," Occasional Paper No. 55, 1987. IMF, *Financial Programming and Policy: The Case of Turkey*, 2000.

and public sector reforms.⁶ At the same time, macroeconomic stability had to be achieved with conventional monetary, fiscal, and exchange rate policies. To gain foreign exchange, artificial deflationary policies were implemented to decrease imports and increase exports.

There were many pros and cons of the application of the liberal policies to developing countries. There are several reasons. First, the conditionalities were interventions into the domestic affairs of policies taken by recipient countries. There were sometimes about 200 conditions for one country, which were required to be implemented within three years, the standard time framework of SALs and ESAFs.⁷

Second, liberalizations imply a loss of vested interests of various parties of the countries concerned. There was fierce opposition to policies like the liberalization of imports and that of FDIs. Third, though the economies were already in a critical condition because of debt crises, artificial deflationary policies to reduce the balance of payments (BOP) deficits caused negative impacts on the economies in the short term. In this regard, there was a strong reaction even from poor dwellers who suffered from cuts in governmental subsidies to essential commodities including food (e.g., Zambia and Indonesia).

The most serious debt crises happened in Latin America. Though the size of the nonperforming debt was small, the crises occurred around the African continent as well. It was reported that the two continents had "lost decades" in the 1980s. Thanks to the introduction of various debt repayment measures, many Latin American countries could get out of the debt crises in the 1990s.

It was Africa that could not escape from this debt even after the continuation of the implementation of SAPs. There were many low-income countries in the region that could not reestablish their economies so that they could pay back arrears of debt and return to international capital

---

⁶Toye, J., "Structural Adjustment: Context, Assumptions, Origin and Diversity," Van der Hoeven, R., & Van der Kraaij, F. (eds) *Structual Adjustment and Beyond in Sub-Saharan Africa*, Ministry of Foreign Affairs, the Hague, 1994. World Bank, *World Bank Guide 2005*.
⁷Both the objectives and measures are published as IMF' policy intentions documents like letters of intent and Memoranda of Economic and Financial Policies for many countries.

markets. There were many reports on the negative impact of SAPs on the African countries.[8]

At that time, the donors behind this framework were the U.S., the U.K., and other European countries.[9] Though Japan opposed some parts of the approach initially, it was obliged to take this approach as a member of G7 and of DAC/OECD. This opposition will be discussed in Chapter 2. It should be noted here that Japan was not in favor of strict conditions of aid. The country favored consultations rather than conditions.

Though discussed in Chapter 3, China, as a developing country, does not take this approach even today. China gives enormous amounts of aid outside this framework.

In this context, as will be discussed in detail in Chapter 3, China's avoidance of the imposition of conditions for aid was welcomed by African governments. It is interesting that Tanzania was host to a large Chinese project, the Tazara (Tanzania–Zambia) Railway, in the 1970s and nowadays occupies an important position in China's maritime route called "String of Pearls." At the same time, Tanzania was a front runner for donor support to government budgets and their common basket funds which will be explained in Section 1.1.2. Though Japan negatively viewed this Western-style aid intervention, it gave budget support to Tanzania since 2004.

1.1.2 Revolutionary Aid Reforms

(1) Deepening of Aid Conditionalities

As explained in Section 1.1.1, the SAP introduced policies for aid that were set in the overall framework for the development of the recipient country and its aid coordination. After the end of the Cold War, the effectiveness of aid became an important issue in Western countries. Significant aid reforms were implemented by DAC member countries. In 1996, DAC

---

[8] Even UNESCO published a book called "Adjustment with a Human Face" in 1985. There are case studies in the following report: Mosley, P. *et al.*, *Aid and Power: The World Bank and Policy-Based Lending Volume 2*, Routledge, 1991.

[9] More than 50 percent of voting powers in the IMF and the World Bank were occupied by those Western countries and Japan.

published a new development strategy for the post-Cold War era.[10] A series of reform measures were discussed and implemented.

During the implementation of SAPs, there were many proposals on aid reforms. The first important proposal was a budget support or program support model rather than a project support model. The budget support model would mean that donors provide money to government budgets. The program support model is budget support to some sectors seen as particularly important to the country's economy.

At the levels of BOP, the program support model included loans to address its deficits. SALs were medium-term loans to provide African countries with foreign exchange so that they could import to sustain their economies. Japan was the biggest provider of parallel loans with SALs to African countries. It is important to note that this program loan model was different from the project loan model, which is characterized by loans to individual projects.

The revolutionary nature of the aid system included the introduction of a sector investment program with a common basket fund. After taking measures for overall structural adjustments with SALs, the World Bank introduced program loans to specific sectors, which are known as Sector Adjustment Loans (SECALs).

The sector investment program contains policies for sectoral development, appropriate projects, and aid in the context of an overall development program of a recipient country. The sectors vary from the agricultural sector to the road sub-sector. This implies a more intensive SAP at the sectoral or sub-sectoral level. On the side of donors, an important approach that was developed is that all donors put their aid money into a common basket fund. This results in a common aid budget managed by donors.

All these efforts led to the Paris Declaration in 2005. This indicated that donors provide aid as a group and that their individual aid activities are to be monitored by peer reviews by other DAC donors. Though Japan resisted budget support and common basket funds, in the end it had to obey the principles set by aid-reforming countries, which were led by the U.K. and Scandinavian countries.

---

[10] DAC/OECD, *Shaping the 21st Century: The Contribution of Development Co-operation*, 1996.

The monitoring of aid policies and practices of each donor was intensive, thorough, and detailed. Within the peer reviews, Japan has been criticized for tying its aid to certain conditions.[11] In fact, its conditions were not very restrictive compared with other donor countries. Tied aid is an important part of China's aid, too.

The author had an opportunity to exchange opinions with a manager of an African section of the Department for International Development (DFID) in London in 1998. At that time, the U.K. advocated for aid that was not branded with the national flag ("flag down"). This approach exemplified the common basket fund explained earlier where aid should be coordinated and given as a group. Similarly, no logo of Japanese organizations should be put on a building which is funded by aid. While the author told him that this approach could not indicate that the aid was coming from Japan and that the aid should appeal to tax payers and the public in Japan, he replied, "aid should be given to a recipient, not for the sake of a donor."

China also signed the Paris Declaration. When the author interviewed specialists of AFD in 2010, they told him that China was out of the aid coordination circle and that they did not cooperate with DAC donors at all. The interview took place just before the 15th session of the Conference of the Parties to the United Nations Framework Convention on Climate Change in Copenhagen in December 2013. The same statements were also uttered by experts of the Sahel and West Africa Club of the OECD in Paris.

On the recipient side, there was severe resistance from African countries. As most of the policies involved interventions in domestic affairs and austerity measures severely impacted their economies, both government and civil society responded fervently to the outsiders' intervention. But in situations of debt crises, they had no alternative but to take the bitter prescription of the BWIs to realize debt rescheduling and fresh aid money to sustain their economies in such critical conditions.

---

[11] At a meeting of a donor agency in Tokyo in December 1999, the participants including the author were surprised by a speech made by the then Director of Department for International Development on Japan's aid. In the transcript, she criticized large amounts of the tied aid, calling Japan's aid a "dinosaur."

(2) Addition of Political Condition

In addition to the aforementioned economic conditionalities, it should be noted that since 1989 a political condition has been imposed for aid. It was the U.S. that took this initiative to democratize African politics speedily after the fall of the Berlin Wall. It was reported that the U.K. and France, which had been former colonial powers in Africa, opposed the American move. These past colonial masters were afraid that speedy democratization would cause ethnic and political confrontations within African countries. But the U.S. government imposed this condition at donors' conferences.

At that time, about five countries had multiparty systems in Africa. In five years, only five countries did not initiate a democratic move. Of course, there was fierce opposition to this additional conditionality more than to the economic conditionalities (structural adjustment). So, both economic and political conditions were linked to aid and debt rescheduling and/or cancellation. One of the late-comers to democratization was Malawi. Having stayed in Malawi as a United Nations expert to its government from 1983 to 1987, the author has monitored the trends until the present time. Though the country resisted the democratic move, it had to start the democratization process in 1993.

It is important to understand that there were severe interventions in domestic affairs by the BWIs and Western donors. The past few decades since 1980 in Africa saw serious chaos on both economic and political fronts as well as some progress in their fields.

1.2 From Aid to Private Investment in the 21st Century

1.2.1 *Africa's Buoyant Economy after Debt Cancellation*

The approach of BWIs ended with cancellations of debt by 2005 (details are explained in Section 1.2.2). Japan, which was a late-comer as a donor and developed its economy with government-led strategies, was opposed to the market-oriented approach initiated by Western donors. In a move to prepare the United Nations Millennium Development Goals in 2000, however, Japan and other G7 countries announced that they would cancel their bilateral aid to Africa at the Cologne Summit in 1999. Moreover, with the strong leadership of the Blair administration at the Gleneagles Summit in the U.K., a cancellation of the BWIs' debt to African countries was announced, which included their substantial loans for structural adjustment.

After the cancellation of the debt of Western donors and BWIs by 2005, many African economies recovered through the global financial crisis starting in 2008. There were economic booms thanks to substantial increases in commodity prices of primary goods from Africa. According to IMF's World Economic Outlook, April 2016, annual economic growth rates in 2015–2016 (estimate and projection) were 3.2 percent for the world, and 6.5 percent for Asia and the Pacific. Though IMF projected 3.2 percent for Sub-Saharan Africa (SSA), it masks real pictures of high growth in the continent. The low overall rate reflected low growth rates in South Africa and Nigeria. Many countries like Mozambique, Tanzania and Ghana registered growth rates of more than 7 percent.

According to the *International Debt Statistics 2016*, published by the World Bank in December 2015, net FDI to SSA in 2014 amounted to 26.6 billion U.S. dollars. The size was large compared with the 60 billion U.S. dollars as FDI to East Asia and the Pacific excluding China. To look at Table 1-2, some African countries receive substantial foreign investment comparable to Asian countries.

Table 1-2 Foreign Investment in Major African and Asian Countries

	Population Millions 2014	Per Capita GNI, U.S.$ 2014	FDI Net Inflow, U.S.$ Billions 2013–2014 (Average)	Portfolio Investment U.S.$ Billions 2013–2014 (Average)
Nigeria	178	2,970	5.2	3.3
South Africa	54	6,800	2.0	1.8
Ghana	27	1,590	3.3	
Kenya	45	1,290	0.3	0.6
Ethiopia	97	550	1.1	
Morocco	34	3,070	3.4	
The Philippines	99	3,500	2.0	0.6
Viet Nam	91	1,890	7.7	
Myanmar	53	1,270	1.6	

Sources: For population and income (GNI), World Bank, *World Development Indicators 2016*, April 2016. For investment, World Bank, *International Debt Statistics 2016*, December 2015.

In addition, the World Bank reported SSA's sovereign bond issuance boom. Eleven heavily indebted poor countries (HIPCs), which will be explained in Section 1.2.2, could issue bonds in international capital markets in 2013 and 2014: Gabon (1.5 billion U.S. dollars), Ghana (1 billion U.S. dollars), and Mozambique (0.9 billion U.S. dollars) in 2013; Kenya (2 billion U.S. dollars), Ethiopia, Ghana, and Zambia (all three at 1 billion U.S. dollars) in 2015.[12]

Thus, the weight of private flows rose to the same level as official aid. ODA to SSA by DAC countries of the OECD amounted to 26.8 billion U.S. dollars (net) in 2013. As stated earlier, FDI in 2014 was 26.6 billion U.S. dollars. It could also be noted that low-income countries like Malawi received higher levels of FDI, too.

1.2.2 Failure of a New Aid Regime?

There has been a long history of structural adjustment led by the U.S., the U.K., and other European countries. Japan, though reluctant, followed suit. Starting in 1980, when the World Bank provided SALs, many African countries were forced to institute neoliberal policies. Though the IMF introduced SAF and ESAF in the mid-1980s, it was realized that the low-income countries in the region were unable to re-establish their economies to pay back external debt accumulated during the boom periods of the 1970s. In the 1990s, democratization of political structures also became a condition for aid. BWIs were concerned only with economic conditionalities, while the U.S. put pressures on African countries for a speedy shift to a multiparty system.

To save low-income countries from undergoing structural adjustment, the Heavily Indebted Poor Countries (HIPC) Initiative began in 1996. Most of the countries were African. This was a system to reschedule external debt drastically if structural adjustments were made. At first, the BWIs and the Western donors believed that the countries concerned would be

---

[12] World Bank, *International Debt Statistics 2016*, p. 13. In addition, "In several countries, the rapid rise in outstanding external debt is attributable to large bond issuance in international capital markets." This statement is cited in World Bank, *International Debt Statistics 2017*, p. 9.

able to get out of the crises in the system. In the end, G7 countries had to announce a cancellation of their bilateral debts in 1999. It was also a prerequisite for the MDGs for those countries to be debt free, which were announced in 2000.

Japan was also obliged to cancel its enormous debt, which included program loans in parallel with the World Bank's SALs. In addition, Japan contributed significantly to special funds for Africa in the World Bank and a fund for ESAF in the IMF. At the behest of the U.K. and other Western donors, the amount of debt that Japan had to write off included its bilateral project aid.

Moreover, at the Gleneagles Summit in the U.K. in 2005, thanks to Tony Blair's initiative, G7 countries agreed to a cancellation of debt by the IMF and the World Bank. The debt of the African Development Bank was also cancelled. Initially, the U.S. did not agree with the cancellation. Blair made substantial contributions to the realization of the cancellation.[13] Their loans to support SAPs also had to be cancelled.

In this sense, the SAP mechanism for low-income countries in Africa since the early 1980s has ended in failure. But there are some tangible results of the activities when one considers the African countries at present.

What is important first is that this link of aid to policy reforms set by the BWIs and Western countries is the approach that is currently being used. Aid is given on the condition of countries liberalizing their economic policies. It is a success for the donors in that debt-ridden countries are put under the control of the BWIs and Western countries, which can request them to take neoliberal policies to the benefit of the donors.

The liberalization of markets has been introduced in most African countries the same way as in other parts of the developing world. Following government-led development strategies, they were faced with inefficiency and loss of competition. Even if there are many low-income countries in Africa at low levels of development, policies like import liberalization and

---

[13] Elliot, L. and A. Seager, "£30bn debts write-off agreed: G7 package brokered by chancellor will benefit 18 of world's poorest countries immediately," *The Guardian*, Saturday June 11, 2005. The report states that "Writing off the multilateral debts of poor countries has been one of Britain's priorities for its presidency of the G8, and today's deal will be seen as a triumph for Mr Brown, who has cajoled sometimes reluctant G7 countries — the G8 minus Russia — to back his plan."

liberalization of capital markets were enforced. Most African countries that opposed the whole system are now very liberal countries.

Following the aid reforms since the mid-1990s, moreover, there have been dramatic changes in aid. Considering SAPs led by the BWIs, there were the following changes in systems of economic cooperation and aid:

(1) One important objective of the SAP was sustainable growth that encouraged private investment, both domestic and foreign. Private flows from abroad were welcome. This means the reduction of reliance on official resources and, in particular, on ODA. What is important is that the amount of ODA should be reduced relative to private flows.
(2) ODA should be used for poor countries, social development, and poverty reduction. Therefore, Africa becomes a priority region. The mode of aid should be grants.

With debt cancellations announced in 1999 and 2005, African countries have enjoyed high growth rates mainly in high commodity prices since 2008 and due to the liberal policies, which attracted foreign investment to their economies.

An additional phenomenon is that major DAC countries also take this opportunity to invest in Sub-Saharan Africa via private enterprises as well as development banks. Though this book focuses on the contest in aid to Africa by Japan and China, many Western donors now take their own nationalistic approaches to invest in African countries. The loans of the development banks may correspond to OOF. The Abe administration, established in late 2012, is active in providing OOF as well as ODA. China is a champion when it comes to providing substantial loans by development banks like the China EXIM. They can have a free hand with OOF against ODA with various reforms.

In recent years, there are reports that new aid regimes in many African countries are not effective because of inflows of private capital and enormous amounts of investment by emerging donors championed by China. Even if there are various policies for sectoral investment programs with common basket funds, many Western donors do not take them seriously and go their own ways. It has happened even in Kenya where donor coordination meetings do not bind aid policies of the donors concerned.

Regarding the mode of aid, European countries believed poor countries should be given grants. The Japanese stance was different in that grants harm self-help efforts and increase aid dependence; Japan also believed that loans are a favored means that can nurture self-help efforts. This issue will be discussed in Chapter 2. This stance can be said to be shared by the Chinese as well.

In general, China's approach is different in that it does not set conditions. Japan followed the new regime introduced by the U.S. and others through the BWIs, though it was reluctant to do so. The policies of the two Asian giants will be discussed in the subsequent chapters: Chapter 2 for Japan and Chapter 3 for China.

Finally, when one thinks about the new aid regime based on efforts of the SAPs since the early 1980s and their achievements and failures, the author would like to stress the following points regarding the important characteristics of the new system of development and aid in Africa to understand the current situations and their futures:

(1) The country approach is the basis for any donor support and private investment in Africa and other developing countries. Specialists of the IMF and the World Bank prepare the overall framework of development and foreign investment and aid by consulting the recipient country. One should note that based on Article IV of IMF, consultations should be made for all countries, even the U.S., Japan, and China.
(2) In relation to the above country or macro approach, coordination of aid and economic cooperation is important. Whether coordination constrains intervention by any donor or investor to a large extent is a good topic for further investigation. But some coordination or understanding of coordination in the context of the country approach is important so that the recipient country can avoid any debt crisis or shortages of foreign exchange and can invest in the development of the country.

One could oppose strict aid coordination and liberalization of markets, which is the main part of neoliberalism initiated by Margaret Thatcher and Ronald Reagan. But the aid system discussed in Section 1.1 should be borne in mind when thinking about development and aid for Sub-Saharan Africa in relation to involvement by Japan and China.

Chapter 2

Aid to Sub-Saharan Africa by Japan

In this chapter, Japan's aid to Sub-Saharan Africa will be summarized. An analysis will be made of the performance of substantial increase in aid and Japan's aid policies. These policies have shifted from the independent policies of a singular Asian donor to assimilation into Western aid frameworks. In addition, Japan's path to becoming a global donor will be analyzed and criticism against Japan's "cash diplomacy" during the Gulf War in 1991 will be investigated.

The author focuses on the differences between Western and Japanese approaches to aid, with the latter being a relative newcomer in this domain. China referred to these differences when it planned aid policies. The author's interviews with Chinese scholars and experts will be presented in Chapter 3.

Section 2.1 will deal with the performance of aid to developing countries in general terms as well as in terms specific to SSA. Trends and achievements of aid until the early 21st century will be analyzed with substantive data. In Section 2.2, these trends and achievements will be analyzed from the early 21st century until today.

2.1 From Asian Donor to Western Donor

Japan's performance with respect to aid will be analyzed in Section 2.1.1 in the context of the overall economy, international economic relations, and economic cooperation, which includes aid or ODA. This is because aid may have been given in relation to trade and investment. Policies for the overall economy and economic relations will also be discussed, while those for economic cooperation will be dealt with in Section 2.1.2.

2.1.1 *Toward Becoming the No. 1 Donor for 10 Years*

(1) Overall Economic Trends

Japan became the second-largest economy in the capitalist world in 1968 when its gross domestic product (GDP) surpassed that of West Germany. Its status as the second-largest economy after the U.S. was lost to China in 2010, about 40 years later. Table 2-1 shows economic comparisons between Japan and China. While China grew at an annual average of about 10 percent for 20 years until 2010, the Japanese economy plummeted during the "Lost Decade," registering about 1 percent on average during the 1990s.

Japan, which held its first Olympic Games in Tokyo in 1964, will host its second Olympic Games in 2020. Shinkansen, or bullet trains, commenced its operations (at a maximum speed of 250 km/h) between Tokyo and Osaka just before the start of the 1964 Olympic Games. The games were followed by an International Exposition (EXPO) in Osaka in 1970.

About 40 years later, China mimicked Japan's achievements. The Beijing Olympic Games were held in 2008 concomitant with the inauguration of a super expressway between Beijing and Tianjin (with a maximum speed of more than 300 km/h). Subsequently, an EXPO was held in Shanghai in 2010. This 40-year time difference is important to understand and analyze aid interventions by Japan and China (see Chapter 3). Japan is now a leading advanced economy, while China, though the second largest in terms of economic size, is classified as a developing country.

The aforementioned economic achievement was a basis for providing aid to developing countries for two reasons. First, Japan became an important provider of financial aid. This point is different from that of Western donors. Second, Japan stressed its path from a developing to a developed country. This second point is related to technical aid. With its experiences as a developing country in Asia, Japan has implemented third-country technical assistance. This economic achievement and the resulting implications for aid were reflected in China's aid (see Chapter 3).

Table 2-1 Macro-Economic Performance of Japan and China

	1990	2000	2008	2009	2010	2016	1991–2000	2001–2010	2011–2016
JAPAN									
Nominal GDP Bn U.S. dollars	3,058	4,667	4,880	5,033	5,459	6,540			
Real GDP Growth rate, %	5.6	2.9	−1.2	−6.3	3.9	1.2	1.2	0.7	1.5
			(over previous year)					(period average)	
Exchange rate Yen per U.S. dollar	144.8	107.8	103.4	93.6	87.8				
			(annual average)						
CHINA									
Nominal GDP Bn U.S. dollars	390	1,198	4,520	4,991	5,878	11,220			
Real GDP Growth rate, %	3.8	8.4	9.6	9.2	10.3	9.5	10.5	10.5	9.5
			(over previous year)					(period average)	
Exchange rate Yuan per U.S. dollar	4.8	8.3	6.9	6.8	6.8				
			(annual average)						

Sources: IMF, *World Economic Outlook Database April 2011*.
IMF, *International Financial Statistics*, various issues.

(2) International Economic Relations

International economic relations will be analyzed using external trade and direct investment indicators. This analysis corresponds to major items of the balance of payments tables. As China restricted portfolio investment, it will not be dealt with in this book. The following analysis mainly uses data on external trade statistics and the balance of payments in the International Financial Statistics published by the IMF. A reference was made to the World Investment Report by the United Nations Conference on Trade and Development (UNCTAD).

(a) External Trade

Japan's economic success following the end of World War II relied mainly on continuous increases in exports against the backdrop of significant currency appreciation of the yen, which rose from 360 yen per U.S. dollar until 1971 to about 110 yen in recent years. Japan has become a net importer of goods and services only since 2011.

Although Japan's major trading partners were the U.S., China, and other Southeast Asian countries, SSA countries were not important to Japan from an economic perspective. According to external trade statistics of the IMF, shares of exports to Africa, including North Africa, in Japan's exports to the world were 1.4 percent in 1995. Those for SSA were 0.9 percent in 2000, 1.0 percent in 2005, 1.1 percent in 2010, and 1.2 percent in 2014.

Shares of imports from Africa, including North Africa, in Japan's total imports were 1.3 percent in 1995. Those for SSA were 1.3 percent in 2000, 1.5 percent in 2005, and 1.8 percent in 2014. Most of Japan's crude oil comes from the Middle East and not from SSA. China's shares of imports and exports with Africa were slightly larger during this period (see Section 3.1.1).

However, Japan relied on imports of materials and energy from abroad and resorted to SSA as an alternate source. There were significant imports of precious metals and other mineral resources from South Africa despite its apartheid policies. On the African side, Table 2-2 shows that Japan's shares were small compared with those of the U.S. and China. China's shares will be discussed in Section 3.1.1.

(b) Foreign Direct Investment (FDI)

Japan has become an important investing country along with traditional Western countries in the world. But its investments are concentrated in the U.S.,

Table 2-2 Principal Trade Partners of Africa

		China Mainland	United States	Japan
		Share in total (%), 2013–2014 (avr.)		
Africa (including North Africa)	Exports	13.5	7.2	3.1
	Imports	15.3	5.8	2.2
Nigeria	Exports	2.0	7.4	3.9
	Imports	23.3	10.5	1.2
South Africa	Exports	11.1	7.2	5.6
	Imports	15.5	6.5	3.9

Source: IMF, *Direction of Trade Statistics 2015*.

Table 2-3 Foreign Direct Investment (FDI) by Japan and China

	2000	2001	2002	2003	2004	2005	2006	2007	2008	2009	2010
FDI (IFS NET ASSETS)											
Billion U.S. dollars											
Japan	31.5	38.5	32.0	28.8	40.6	51.7	58.2	73.0	113.6	73.7	79.7
China	0.9	6.9	2.5	−0.2	8.0	13.7	23.9	17.2	56.7	43.9	58.0

	2011	2012	2013	2014	2015
FDI (IFS NET ASSETS)					
Billion U.S. dollars					
Japan	116.8	117.6	155.7	136.3	130.7
China	48.4	65.0	73.0	123.1	187.8

Source: IMF, *International Financial Statistics*.

China, and Southeast Asian countries. Table 2-3 shows trends of FDI by Japan and China. Japan exited the "Lost Decade" around 2003 and has increased FDI since then. FDI levels have reached more than 100 billion U.S. dollars since 2011. The latest developments in FDI will be discussed in Section 2.2.1.

Africa's shares are marginal. Table 2-4 shows that only South Africa received significant amounts of investment from Japan. Top enterprises like Toyota Motors have their factories in South Africa. One can easily

Table 2-4 Japan's Relationships with Africa

Country	FDI (Mn U.S.$) 2014	Japanese Companies Oct-14	Japanese Residents 1-Oct-14	Residents in Japan 31-Dec-14
Angola	—	2	71	60
Benin	—	—	72	70
Botswana	—	1	79	50
Burkina Faso	—	—	133	72
Burundi	—	—	19	16
Cabo Verde	—	—	2	7
Cameroon	—	—	74	521
Central African Republic	—	—	4	20
Chad	—	—	7	2
Comoros	—	—	0	2
Democratic Republic of the Congo	—	—	59	369
Republic of Congo	—	—	7	27
Côte d'Ivoire	—	2	80	164
Djibouti	—	—	49	27
Equatorial Guinea	—	—	15	1
Eritrea	—	—	1	28
Ethiopia	—	1	254	414
Gabon	—	—	65	40
The Gambia	—	—	8	41
Ghana	—	6	339	2,061
Guinea	—	—	18	345
Guinea-Bissau	—	—	2	6
Kenya	—	6	769	678
Lesotho	—	—	4	15
Liberia	—	9	7	49
Madagascar	—	2	91	118
Malawi	—	1	173	84
Mali	—	—	21	154

(*Continued*)

Table 2-4 (Continued)

Country	FDI (Mn U.S.$) 2014	Japanese Companies Oct-14	Japanese Residents 1-Oct-14	Residents in Japan 31-Dec-14
Mauritania	—	—	19	12
Mauritius	—	3	40	132
Mozambique	—	4	179	90
Namibia	—	—	65	25
Niger	—	1	10	19
Nigeria	—	12	141	2,671
Rwanda	—	—	116	78
São Tomé e Príncipe	—	—	0	2
Senegal	—	2	228	461
Seychelles	—	—	12	5
Sierra Leone	—	—	11	36
Somalia	—	—	1	16
South Africa	1,688.69	66	1,377	899
South Sudan	—	—	429	9
Sudan	—	—	138	300
Swaziland	—	1	16	7
Tanzania	—	3	350	431
Togo	—	—	2	42
Uganda	—	2	279	533
Zambia	—	2	252	158
Zimbabwe	—	3	86	136

Source: Ministry of Foreign Affairs, *Country Handbook 2016*.

understand the little investment in Africa by Japanese enterprises. A similar table on China's presence in Africa will be presented and discussed in Section 3.1.1.

Because of economic difficulties in SSA in the 1980s and 1990s, many Japanese multinational corporations (MNCs) withdrew their investments from the region during these two decades. They had invested for import substitution in sectors like electronics in some English-speaking countries like Kenya and Tanzania. They have since recovered following debt relief in 2005 (see Section 2.2.1).

Based on past trends, SSA was not important for the Japanese economy. Relationships of trade and FDI were marginal for Japan. This implies that Japan's engagement in SSA is not for economic profit but rather for political or philanthropic purposes. There may be three purposes. First, sharing the values of G7 countries, Japan increased ODA for the sake of development and poverty reduction of developing countries in SSA. Humanitarian rationales underpin the reason for their aid.

Second, Japan also wanted to be an influential country or a global partner engaged in all important issues around the world. Third, it is also said that the government gives aid to SSA so that the countries vote for Japan's application for a permanent seat in the Security Council of the United Nations.

Finally, it could be added that the countries in Southeast Asia were major recipients of Japan's ODA. The assistance was linked to trade and investment in those countries. Western criticism of the commercial nature of Japan's ODA in Asian countries is true for those countries but not for Africa. Japan's ODA presence in Southeast Asia is still very high.

(3) Economic Cooperation and Aid

(a) Economic Cooperation

As in Chapter 3 on China, economic cooperation will be explained first; then its components, namely, ODA and Other Official Flow (OOF), will be discussed. Table 2-5 shows economic cooperation, which includes ODA. Japan's ODA is compared with those of the U.K. and the U.S. The U.K. is known as a forerunner of aid reforms in major European countries. The Blair administration took significant initiatives. The new institution, the Department of International Development implemented a number of measures like the common basket fund.

The U.S. is a major donor in the world. The amounts of Japan's ODA surpassed those of the U.S. for 10 years, chiefly in the 1990s, toppling the U.S. in 1989. That year saw the highest stock index price (Nikkei Average) in one of the most buoyant economic booms. In 1999, the net ODA expenditure of Japan was 15.3 billion U.S dollars against the 9.2 billion U.S. dollars by the U.S. The U.S. was not as active in aid reforms at that

Table 2-5 Economic Cooperation by Major Donors (Million US$)

	Japan					United Kingdom					United States				
	2004-05	2012	2013	2014	2015	2004-05	2012	2013	2014	2015	2004-05	2012	2013	2014	2015
NET DISBURSEMENTS															
I. Official Development Assistance (ODA) (A + B)	11,024	10,605	11,469	9,483	9,203	9,338	13,891	17,871	19,306	18,545	23,820	30,652	31,267	33,096	30,986
ODA as % of GNI	0.23	0.17	0.22	0.20	0.21	0.42	0.56	0.70	0.70	0.70	0.20	0.19	0.18	0.19	0.17
A. Bilateral Official Development Assistance	8,151	6,402	8,499	6,129	6,147	6,765	8,665	10,545	11,233	11,710	20,916	25,423	26,360	27,509	26,654
of which: General budget support	174	-297	2,122	-39	-146	568	349	211	87	76	233	378	584	177	288
Core support to national NGOs	189	114	99	97	100	412	320	329	394	326	—	25	—	5	1
Investment projects	2,023	2,071	756	2,111	2,116	501	627	1,113	916	2,153	2,221	241	445	335	505
Administrative costs	686	794	653	630	603	468	528	370	432	650	1,044	2,172	2,178	1,974	2,120
Other in-donor expenditures (a)	1	4	4	3	2	14	64	59	226	387	519	832	977	1,246	1,202
of which: Refugees in donor countries	—	1	1	1	—	—	45	51	222	385	519	832	977	1,246	1,202
Imputed student costs	—	—	—	—	—	—	—	—	—	1	—	—	—	—	—
B. Contributions to Multilateral Institutions	2,873	4,202	2,970	3,355	3,055	2,574	5,226	7,326	8,073	6,835	2,904	5,230	4,906	5,586	4,331
of which: UN	1,174	679	593	596	424	448	705	685	855	672	587	941	898	895	909
EU	—	—	—	—	—	1,356	1,852	1,907	1,922	2,027	—	—	—	—	—
IDA	757	1,401	1,139	1,049	1,445	456	1,173	1,853	2,702	1,826	1,298	1,492	1,351	1,360	1,288
Regional Development Banks	469	969	768	796	492	79	409	414	464	433	344	699	506	588	529

(*Continued*)

Table 2-5 (Continued)

	Japan					United Kingdom					United States				
	2004–05	2012	2013	2014	2015	2004–05	2012	2013	2014	2015	2004–05	2012	2013	2014	2015
II. Other Official Flows (OOF) Net (C + D)	-2,396	5,393	1,286	-899	-1,055	-127	36	187	41	—	-864	2,462	1,427	210	-43
C. Bilateral Other Official Flows (1 + 2)	-1,715	6,206	1,505	-899	-1,055	-127	36	187	41	—	-864	2,462	1,427	210	-43
1. Official export credits (b)	-666	-530	-353	37	53	29	15	127	—	—	-1,249	2,386	1,630	180	-542
2. Equities and other bilateral assets	-1,049	6,736	1,858	-936	-1,108	-156	21	59	41	—	386	76	-203	30	499
D. Multilateral Institutions	-682	-813	-219	—	—	—	—	—	—	—	—	—	—	—	—
III. Grants by Private Voluntary Agencies	340	487	458	467	498	558	1,025	1,016	—	—	7,710	27,198	25,867	25,998	28,816
IV. Private Flows at Market Terms (Long-Term) (1 to 4)	8,335	32,494	45,133	31,667	28,877	21,716	48,508	11,664	12,462	—	42,238	107,194	93,299	179,345	-21,239
1. Direct investment	11,822	31,215	38,715	27,329	25,800	16,452	40,602	—	—	—	20,063	46,433	36,418	40,238	25,288
2. Private export credits	-883	-3,951	3,271	-736	2,694	-491	1,479	-411	-299	—	-196	4,149	787	262	10,500
3. Bilateral portfolio investment	-1,134	6,470	4,859	6,254	191	5,754	6,427	12,075	12,761	—	22,216	58,066	47,036	136,394	-65,113
4. Securities of multilateral agencies	-1,469	-1,241	-1,712	-1,180	193	—	—	—	—	—	156	-1,454	9,058	2,451	8,086
V. Total Resource Flows (Long-Term) (I to IV)	17,303	48,977	58,346	40,718	37,524	31,485	63,461	30,738	31,809	18,545	72,904	167,506	151,860	238,648	38,520
Total Resource Flows as a % of GNI	0.37	0.80	1.14	0.85	0.87	1.41	2.57	1.21	1.16	0.70	0.61	1.01	0.88	1.34	0.21

Source: OECD, Development Co-operation Report 2015.

Table 2-6 Foreign Aid by Japan and China

	2004	2005	2006	2007	2008	2009	2010	2011	2012	2013	2014	2015
Japan's Foreign Aid												
Net Exp., Billion U.S. dollars												
Bilateral ODA	6.0	10.5	7.4	5.8	6.9	6.1	7.4	6.5	6.4	8.5	6.1	6.1
Total ODA	9.0	13.3	11.3	7.7	9.7	9.6	11.1	10.8	10.6	11.5	9.4	9.2
Total OOF	−3.0	−2.4	3.1	0.7	0.0	11.4	5.6	4.5	5.9	2.1	−0.2	0.0
China's Bilateral Aid												
(External Assistance)												
Gross Exp., Billion U.S. dollars	0.8	0.9	1.0	1.5	1.8	1.9	2.0	2.5	2.6	2.8	3.0	
% change over prev. yr	20.6	19.8	13.3	41.9	26.2	5.2	3.3	22.5	7.4	4.0	9.3	
Gross Exp., 10,000 Yuan	60.7	74.7	82.4	111.5	128.5	133.0	136.1	159.1	166.9	170.5	184.6	
% change over prev. yr	16.2	23.1	10.3	35.4	15.2	3.4	2.4	16.9	4.9	2.2	8.2	
FDI (IFS NET ASSETS)												
Billion U.S. dollars												
Japan	40.6	51.7	58.2	73.0	113.6	73.7	79.7	116.8	117.6	155.7	136.3	130.7
China	8.0	13.7	23.9	17.2	56.7	43.9	58.0	48.4	65.0	73.0	123.1	187.8

Sources: Ministry of Foreign Affairs (Japan), *Japan's ODA*, various issues.
National Bureau of Statistics (China), *Statistical Yearbook*, various issues.
IMF, *International Financial Statistics*, various issues.

time. Rather, the country may have competed with Japan as the leading donor in the amounts of ODA and OOF but not in terms of their quality (aid in reforms).

The characteristics of Japan's aid compared with the two other donors are as follows:

(1) Compared with the U.K., Japan's ODA puts more emphasis on projects than on programs (i.e., general budget support). In aid reforms, there has been a shift from project aid to program aid. As explained in Section 1.1.2, project aid without coordination with development needs and other donors' aid approaches were given low priority. The U.K. advocated aid in a programmatic manner so that aid was closely linked to the needs of recipient countries and duplication of aid by donors and dependence on aid could be avoided. Most of China's aid is project aid.
(2) Japan's ODA may have the same tendency as that of the U.S. in project aid. The share of project aid by the U.S. is high compared to that of the U.K. It should be noted, however, that Japan gave significant amounts of general budget support, making Japan a Western-style donor.
(3) The same characteristics can be found in OOF for Japan and the U.S. As stated earlier, the two countries competed to become the top donor. They provided large amounts of loans at high interest rates. China's aid is very large because of huge amounts of OOF (China EXIM Bank) (see Section 3.1.1).

China was one of the largest recipients of Japan's aid. Its ODA to China changed in recent years. Provision of general grants was terminated in 2006 and loans in 2007. Technical cooperation has taken place under a cost-sharing scheme.

Finally, with respect to the sectoral distribution of ODA using financial loans, economic infrastructure was a priority. Other conventional sectoral groups of DAC were direct production sectors and social sectors. Japan used to place an emphasis on direct production sectors like agriculture and manufacturing. This is based on its philosophy of self-help efforts, which will be discussed in Section 2.1.2. Responding to Western aid reforms, however, Japan nowadays gives higher priority to social sectors like education and health. With the adoption of SAPs, direct production sectors and economic infrastructure were left to the private sector.

(b) Official Development Assistance (ODA)
The white paper on ODA in 1989 contained a survey of its ODA history. In *Forty Years of Japan's Official Development Assistance: From a Recipient to the Top Donor-*, this history is presented below:

Period 1 (1945–1953):
Period of Postwar Economic Reconstruction (as a recipient of economic assistance from the U.S. and the World Bank).

Period 2 (1954–1963).
Period of Postwar Reparations (beginning of provision of foreign aid as payment of reparations).

Period 3 (1964–1976):
Period of Aid Expansion (quantitative expansion and diversification of types of assistance).

Period 4 (1977–1988):
Period of Systematic Aid Expansion (expansion of aid by setting up medium-term targets).

Period 5 (1989–Present):
Period of the Top Donorship (taking initiative as the top donor).

As the latest developments in China's economic powers and its economic cooperation and aid are spectacular, it is worth paying attention to Japan's most recent period. The policies will be discussed in Section 2.1.2.

As regards geographical distribution, Table 2-7 shows the top-10 recipients of Japan's ODA. Asian countries were major recipients. It was long said that 60 percent went to Asia and another 10 percent was given to SSA, Latin America, and the Middle East. With strong economic ties, China and countries in Southeast Asia were important for Japan. They were major trade partners for both exports and imports. Japanese enterprises invested massive amounts in the region, which were second only to their investments in the American market.

Table 2-7 Top Recipients of Japan's ODA

	2001–2002 (Av. Value)	2007–2008 (Av. Value)	2008–2011 (Av. Value)
1	China	Iraq	Viet Nam
2	India	China	India
3	Thailand	Indonesia	Indonesia
4	Indonesia	India	Afghanistan
5	Philippines	Viet Nam	China
6	Viet Nam	Philippines	Congo, Dem. Rep.
7	Bangladesh	Bangladesh	Pakistan
8	Pakistan	Tanzania	The Philippines
9	Sri Lanka	Turkey	Sri Lanka
10	Brazil	Sri Lanka	Iraq

Source: OECD, *Development Co-operation Report*, various issues.

Regarding the mode of ODA, grant elements are high, reflecting an emphasis on low-income countries. What is important is that grant aid is tied to Japanese companies, which was always criticized in OECD Peer Reviews on Japan's ODA.[1] Technical assistance, which is mostly given with grants, is also tied to Japanese enterprises. But this tied aid is also a phenomenon of some major donors like the U.S. It is also a characteristic of China's aid interventions.

In addition to private funds (FDI and portfolio investment), ODA was important in the context of Japan's economic and diplomatic policies. Despite the Lost Decade in the 1990s, Japan became the leading provider of ODA for 10 years starting in 1989. Because of persistent economic depression, Japan's ODA has declined since then (see Table 2-6).

(c) Other Official Flow (OOF)

As will be discussed in Chapter 3 for China, the role of OOF has become very important. This is because infrastructure projects promoted by Japan and China require large amounts of money. In addition, the countries can

---

[1] The Peer Reviews on Japan were made by other DAC member countries in 1995, 2003, 2010, and 2014.

Table 2-8 Development Banks

	Capital (100 Million U.S. Dollars)
China Export-Import Bank (EXIM)	8
China Development Bank (CDB)	488
Japan Bank for International Cooperation (JBIC)	157
Asian Infrastructure Investment Bank (AIIB)	500
Asian Development Bank	1,635
World Bank (IBRD)	2,232

Notes: 2014 for AIIB and BRICS. 2013 for IBRD. 2012 for others.
Source: Routledge, Europa World Year Book, 2014

take a free hand when providing OOF, while ODA may be more subject to Western aid practices.

As explained in (a) on "Economic Cooperation" earlier, OOF is important in Japan's economic cooperation. Table 2-8 delineates important official development banks in Japan and China (see Chapter 3 on China).

Japan Bank for International Development (JBIC) was established in 1999 as a merger between the Japan Export-Import Bank (EXIM) and the Overseas Economic Cooperation Fund (OECF). There was a long history of institutional reforms of governmental banks. The reforms were linked to budget reforms of the central government. China has a China EXIM, which plays very important roles in the country's aid to developing countries. China has not had any such financial reforms.

Japan EXIM was established in 1950 as a governmental bank to promote external trade. The bank provided export credit and high-interest loans. Those amounts were captured in OOF. The bank played an important role in recycling its trade surplus in the 1980s and 1990s. There were Japan–U.S. strategic talks in the late 1980s and early 1990s. The U.S. requested Japan to return foreign reserves amassed through exports to international communities.

OECF was established in 1961 as a governmental bank to promote ODA. The bank provided low-interest loans. These concessional loans are included in ODA. The bank took the same role as Japan EXIM to recycle the trade surplus. Its financial loans contributed to an increase in Japan's ODA. As a late-comer donor, Japan had to resort to financial loans in large amounts rather than technical assistance. The country lacked technical expertise in relation to developing countries in the South. OECF's loans were administered by the following three governmental ministries and an agency: the Ministry of Foreign Affairs (MOFA), the Ministry of Finance, the Ministry of International Trade and Industry (MITI), and the Economic Planning Agency (EPA) of the Prime Minister's Office.[2] MITI was involved in the promotion of external trade and in export promotion in particular. In the case of China, the most important aid agency is the Ministry of Commerce (see Section 3.2.2).

Japan EXIM and OECF were first merged into one institution, though each of the two made independent operations. High-interest loans were provided by the EXIM, while ODA loans were provided by the OECF. It should be noted that the provision of grants was planned and implemented by the MOFA. OOF loans were administered by the aforementioned ministries and agency.

Further reforms were implemented in the 21st century. The institutional reforms of governmental banks were implemented during Prime Minister Junichiro Koizumi's regime (2001–2006). Though his cold relationship with China will be discussed in Chapter 4, it was he who wanted to restructure government budgets and financing. As a popular politician, he pursued his policy to privatize the governmental Postal Savings Bank. This bank had squeezed Japan's financial markets and provided financial sources for Japan EXIM and OECF as well as domestic development banks.

In fact, substantial governmental institutional reforms were implemented in 2001. There were mergers of some ministries and agencies. Formal evaluation systems of governmental works and business were introduced. The financial reforms, which are called Japan's "Big Bang,"[3] had been implemented from 1997 to 2001. The last reform was the privatization of governmental banks. The agenda was taken up seriously by

---

[2] MITI is currently the Ministry of Economy, Trade and Industry, which also includes the EPA since 2001.
[3] The U.K. started its financial reform in 1986. It was called "Big Bang."

Prime Minister Koizumi. In the face of strong opposition to the privatization of the Postal Savings Bank, Koizumi experienced an overwhelming victory in the legislative election in 2003.

It was in 2008 that JBIC was reorganized as a successor to Japan EXIM. OECF activities were handed over to Japan International Cooperation Agency (JICA). JICA had been established in 1974 as an agency of technical assistance under the administrative control of MOFA. Since the establishment of JBIC, JICA has had a hand in providing financial assistance at low interest. The provision of grants stayed in the hands of MOFA but more related activities were handed over to JICA.

At present, JBIC plays very important roles in Japan's economic cooperation. The loans and export credits are captured in OOF. The government can exert a free hand as opposed to ODA, which is constrained by Western aid reforms. The bank's role is also important in African countries and other developing countries, which have enjoyed growth led by private enterprises after debt crises in the 1990s.

There was an official trade insurance institution to provide insurance for export finance. China has a similar organization. Japan's Nippon Export and Investment Insurance (NEXI) became a private company in April 2017. Privatization of governmental banking and insurance activities was taken seriously in Japan. This may not have happened in China. The Chinese official banks play important roles in China's economic cooperation and aid.

As Japan has undergone the reforms explained above, JBIC and others cannot take on very risky projects, which may happen with frequency in Africa. In China's case, sizable amounts of loans can be disbursed because there is support from the government, which is backed by the Communist Party.

(d) Contribution at Multilateral Levels

There was contribution of aid by Japan to Africa at multilateral levels, too. The initiative was taken by the Ministry of Finance. Japan has been the second-largest contributor to capital of the BWIs.

The World Bank created a special fund for African countries in the 1980s. As requested by the U.S. and other Western donors, Japan was the biggest contributor to this fund. Supporting SAP, moreover, Japan provided parallel loans with SALs of the World Bank for several African countries.

At the same time, Japan was a major contributor to the increase in capital of the World Bank and the IMF so that they could provide more loans to developing countries. Japan contributed to the two institutions of the World Bank, namely, the International Bank for Reconstruction and Development (IBRD) and the International Development Association (IDA), which provide concessional loans. The IMF created a special fund called ESAF. Many of the countries eligible for the loans were African. This move was a supplement to the World Bank's SALs since 1980. Japan provided 40 percent of the initial fund of the ESAF. There was an overwhelming presence by Japan at that time.

2.1.2 *Opposition to the "Washington Consensus" in Africa*

(1) Policies for Economic Cooperation and Aid
Japanese aid policies have represented an interaction between its independent policies and its forced adoption of Western aid reforms. As a late-comer for assisting developing countries, Japan tried to distinguish itself from Western donors based on its own development experience up until the 1980s.

As explained in Section 2.1.1, Japan was a developing donor. As there was not an accumulation of experiences in developing countries by Japan, financial aid was given higher priority than technical aid.

To look at the history of aid policies, in a publication titled *The Philosophies of Economic Cooperation: Why Official Development Assistance?* issued in 1980, the MOFA stated that Japan's economic cooperation is guided by two motives: "humanitarian and moral considerations" and "the recognition of interdependence among nations."[4] These two motives are reflected in the first ODA Charter in 1992, which is explained later.

To focus on the period in which Japan became a top donor in the 1980s, as stated in the history in Section 2.1.1, it is important to look at the first ODA Charter, which was decided by the Cabinet on June 30,

---

[4] Japan's Ministry of Foreign Affairs, "The White Paper on Japan's ODA 1994," p. 21.

Table 2-9 Japan's ODA Charter 1992

BASIC PHILOSOPHY
(1) The imperative of humanitarian considerations.
(2) Recognition of the interdependent relationships among member nations of the international community.
(3) The necessity for conserving the environment.
(4) The necessity for supporting self-help effort of developing countries.

PRINCIPLES
(1) Environmental conservation and development should be pursued in tandem.
(2) Any use of ODA for military purposes or for aggravation of international conflicts should be avoided.
(3) Full attention should be paid to trends in recipient countries' military expenditures, their development and production of mass destruction weapons and missiles, their export and import of arms, etc., so as to maintain and strengthen international peace and stability, and from the viewpoint that developing countries should place appropriate priorities in the allocation of their resources in their own economic and social development.
(4) Full attention should be paid to efforts for promoting democratization and introduction of a market-oriented economy, and the situation regarding the securing of basic human rights and freedoms in the recipient country.

Source: Ministry of Foreign Affairs, *Japan's ODA Annual Report 1997 and 1999*.

1992. The Charter comprises basic policy, principles, priority, measures, and other sections. The basic policy has four "philosophical underpinnings" (or pillars) presented in Table 2-9.

As explained in Table 2-9, the first two pillars were the initial two motives for aid. The fourth and last pillar, "The necessity for supporting self-help efforts of developing countries," was often cited as a major philosophy in other government documents. Japan's aid philosophy was a self-help effort.

There are remarks by Professor S. Pharre of Harvard University on *The White Paper on Japan's ODA 1989* (in Japanese) by Japan's MOFA. She stated in a subcommittee on Asia and the Pacific of the Committee of the U.S. House of Representatives in September 1988 that an important characteristic of Japan's approach to aid was its experience of economic self-reliance as a developing country. Thus, Japan's philosophy may be different from Western philosophy based on Christian benevolence. More emphasis on loans than grants, and passive views on debt relief may be based on its belief about how a nation should be developed.

The second pillar of the Charter was often criticized by Western donors and critics within Japan, which paid attention to the link between official aid and private commercial activities, namely, trade and investment. Some call this a three-pronged approach. This approach was cited by a Chinese scholar as a lesson for China (the author's interview with the Chinese scholar will be presented in Chapter 3).

However, it should be noted that the link may have been there for Asia but not for Africa. As explained in Section 2.1.1, SSA was not important for Japan's trade and investment. Western criticism against large amounts of Japan's ODA may have mattered for Asia but not mattered much for SSA.

The first Charter has the "Principles" section after the section on "Basic Philosophy." They are listed in Table 2-9. According to the white paper on Japan's ODA in 1994, there are explanations regarding its policies in the Period of the Top Donorship (1989 to present). Those explanations include the four principles in Table 2-9. What is important is the explanation about the environment surrounding Japan: "Following the collapse of the Soviet Union and the Gulf crisis triggered by the Iraqi invasion to Kuwait in 1990, such points as the democratization process of the recipient developing countries, situations of their human rights, military expenditure, and export and import of weapons became focal to the provision of the aid."[5]

Finally, of the aforementioned four, one can pay attention to (4), which talks about, "efforts for promoting democratization and introduction of a market-oriented economy." This means that both political and economic conditions set by the BWIs and Western donors were adopted by Japan.

(2) Opposition to Market-Oriented Approach
As explained in Chapter 1, an important turnaround came in the 1980s. With the advent of liberal (neoclassical) administrations in the U.K. and the U.S. around 1980, a market-oriented approach was taken by the then

---

[5] Japan's Ministry of Foreign Affairs, *The White Paper on Japan's ODA 1994*, p. 21.

debt-ridden developing countries, particularly in Latin America and SSA. SAPs were imposed and implemented by the IMF and the World Bank in most of the countries in need of financial assistance from those BWIs.

Other important components of the adjustment programs were a country-level approach and aid coordination. The former stipulated that BWIs make a macroeconomic forecast considering debt relief and financing needs of the recipient country for all donor countries. Aid coordination was naturally needed in this framework.

Japan was requested by the U.S. and European donors to provide parallel loans to African countries with significant debt relief. Japan opposed the market-oriented approach, what is called the "Washington Consensus" explained in Chapter 1,[6] and outright debt relief because it believed that the program would harm self-help efforts by African countries. The country also feared that it could not pursue independent policies within the framework of the BWIs and aid coordination.

Aid coordination led by European donors finally arrived at the Paris Declaration on Aid Effectiveness in 2005. Though Japan resisted excessive coordination, such as the common basket fund and budget support, it was obliged to follow these new aid procedures as a donor from the developed world.

Agreements on debt relief for heavily indebted poor countries were reached at G7 summit meetings in 1999 and 2005. After providing substantial loans within the framework of adjustment programs, Japan became the largest debtor for African countries. Though the country resisted the move led by Christian organizations, it had no alternative but

---

[6] The OECF presented a paper in which it opposed the World Bank and other international arenas in October 1991. The main points were as follows: (1) only government can take a long-term strategy of the country concerned; (2) without a fostering of industries, the country cannot go up to a higher level of development, especially industrial development; (3) interest rates determined by markets cannot foster small and medium enterprises (SMEs) and help poor farmers. At the initial stages of development, low interest rates subsidized by the government are needed. The last point became an important issue because the OECF provided developing countries with lower interest rates compared with the World Bank's loans. Responding to criticism from the World Bank, the OECF tried to reflect market-determined interest rates and set its rates a little below those set by the World Bank.

to implement outright relief the same way as other donors like the U.K.[7] In addition, Japan had to follow the new aid practices as a G7 member and as a DAC member of the OECD.

2.2 Path to Global Donor

Increasing aid in volume, Japan tried to expand its influence as a global partner. In this section, this new dimension of aid will be presented along with the latest developments of the economy, aid, and policies.

2.2.1 *Tackling Global Issues with the U.S.*

(1) Overall Economy

In the 21st century, the Japanese economy continued to stagnate even after the Lost Decade in the 1990s. This led to high levels of public debt (250% of GDP), the worst among G7 countries. These budgetary difficulties constrained the aid budget (see Table 2-6). Economic recovery came only after the establishment of the Abe administration in December 2012. The trends, including Abenomics, will be explained in Chapter 5.

In addition, ODA's importance declined with more private-led development endorsed by the Seoul Development Consensus for Shared Growth in 2010 at the Group of 20 (G20) summit meeting. As explained in Section 1.2.1, African economies registered high growth rates after the debt cancellation announced in 2005 and high commodity prices from the beginning of the global financial crisis. So, ODAs' importance was linked to poverty reduction. Hence, Africa became a priority region.

(2) International Economic Relations

Regarding external trade, Japan has become a net importer in recent years. With respect to investment, more than 50% of the profits of Japanese MNCs were earned abroad in recent years. Japan is a major investor with enormous remittance of profits to the home country. Asia remained most important for Japan's external trade and FDI. With increases in its

---

[7] At that time, there were many demonstrations by Christian organizations for Japan's debt cancellation outside the Japanese embassy in London. The similar NGO activities were implemented outside the Ministry of Finance in Tokyo.

economy since the establishment of the Abe administration in late 2012, Japan had to resort to Africa as an alternative supplier of mineral resources.

Africa started to grow at high rates after the debt relief in 2005. With high commodity prices since the beginning of the global economic crisis in 2008, moreover, African economies recovered significantly. Some Japanese companies have started to reinvest in Africa. For example, Toyota Tsusho, a trading company of the Toyota Motor group, took over a large French trading company, CFAO. Then, CFAO started to reopen supermarkets of Carrefour, the world's second-largest retail grocery chain, which originated in France.

In addition to traditional investors like Toyota in the transport sectors, new companies are investing in the consumption and service sectors in Africa. In this context, TICAD V in 2013 focused on public–private partnerships. TICAD VI also brought some 200 companies to the conference held in Kenya. Though SSA was important for Japan for political reasons (global partnership), its economic importance has increased since 2008.

(3) Economic Cooperation and Aid

Today, Japan is the world's fourth-largest provider of ODA. In the preceding section, it was reported that Japan retained its leading position in the ODA community in the 1990s, one of the worst economic depressions in history. Looking at ODA statistics for 2015 in detail published by the Foreign Ministry, private funds or flows are more than official monetary flows. Of the official flows, it is important to note large amounts of OOF.

With respect to the mode of economic cooperation and aid, they reflect an emphasis of the Abe administration on OOF and private funds for infrastructure investment and the activities of private enterprises. Financial loans of ODA are also given priority. Only ODA resources were earmarked for Africa and other low-income regions in Asia in conformity with poverty reduction. This is a political demonstration of ODA to cater to MDGs and SDGs. Japan aligns itself with Western donors to earmark ODA for low-income countries, including many African countries, and for social sectors like poverty reduction, a key goal of MDGs and SDGs.

(4) Aid as a Global Partner
Based on its surge of economic powers, Japan, as a G7 member, regards itself as a global partner. Japan's ODA became the largest for the first time in 1989, and it remained the top donor until 1999. Its economic powers and political aspirations based on aid budgets were recognized by the U.S. during two bilateral structural talks in the 1980s and after. Although liberalization of trade and investment was reported in mass media, it is important to understand that the American framework was comprehensive. They included consultations about aid policies. Global Issues Initiatives were announced, which would lead the two countries to joint projects for tackling issues like environmental degradation and health, including Human Immunodeficiency Virus (HIV), at the global level.[8]

This experience may be the reason for Japan's initiative to hold policy talks with China and South Korea for African development. In addition, Japan's bilateral economic dialogue with China included joint action for aid to third countries.

China started its Strategic and Economic Dialogue with the U.S. in 2009, about 20 years later than Japan. Though further exploration surveys are needed about the role of aid policies in the talks, the two countries implemented a joint construction project in Liberia in 2010 (see Chapter 3).

2.2.2 From Defeat in the Gulf War to Initiatives for Fragile States

Another new dimension of Japan's ODA in recent years will be discussed in this section. An important element of this is aid used for political and military purposes in addition to economic ones. In the second half of this section, administrative structures for aid will be summarized.

(1) Policies for Economic Cooperation and Aid
After the debt cancellation in 2005 and commodity price booms under the global financial crisis, the Abe administration used OOF and ODA to support private investment in Africa and other parts of the world.

---

[8] The author participated in a study on HIV commissioned by Japan's Foreign Ministry. The interview was conducted at a USAID office in Bangkok, Thailand, which was selected as a case.

Table 2-10   Development Cooperation Charter 2015

PHILOSOPHY
(1) OBJECTIVES OF DEVELOPMENT COOPERATION
— Japan will promote development cooperation in order to contribute more proactively to the peace, stability and prosperity of the international community.
— ODA, as the core of various activities that contribute to development, will serve as a catalyst for mobilizing a wide range of resources in cooperation with various funds and actors and, by extension, as an engine for various activities aimed at securing peace, stability and prosperity of the international community.

(2) BASIC POLICIES
A. Contributing to peace and prosperity through cooperation for non-military purposes.
B. Promoting human security.
C. Cooperation aimed at self-reliant development through assistance for self-help efforts as well as dialogue and collaboration based on Japan's experience and expertise.

Source: Ministry of Foreign Affairs, *Cabinet Decision on the Development Cooperation Charter*, February, 2015. http://www.mofa.go.jp/files/000067702.pdf (May 28, 2017).

The ODA Charter in 1992 was explained in Section 2.1.2. Its revised version in 2003 was changed under the Abe administration in 2015. The main parts are presented in Table 2-10.

There are three major changes presented as follows:

(1) The ODA Charter was changed for the Development Cooperation Charter. The scope was widened to reflect the importance of OOF and private funds as well as ODA.
(2) Japan's independent policies continued to be sought. Support to "self-help efforts" was rewritten in this new Charter. This has been an important pillar of Japan's ODA and clearly stated in the ODA Charter in 1992.
(3) There is more active link between ODA and Peace Keeping Operation (PKO) activities. With changes in laws in the face of strong opposition, the administration can engage its military personnel in PKO activities more easily.

The administration, which tried to enhance Japan's international status, placed more emphasis on Africa. The latest TICAD meeting was held in Kenya in late August 2016, three years after the conference in Yokohama, Japan, in 2013. This corresponds to China's FOCAC meetings, which have been held every three years since 2000. TICAD had been held every five years from 1993 to 2013 (see Chapter 4).

(2) Aid for Political and Military Purposes
SSA remained important for Japan, which aspired to be a global partner for the MDGs and SDGs. Policies for economic cooperation and aid are part of foreign policies. The former has been increasingly linked to the latter in recent years. Japan cannot be a major military power because of its Constitution prepared under U.S. rule after the end of World War II. Based on its economic success, economic cooperation is the most important measure it can use to demonstrate its interests at the global level.

Further involvement in global political affairs has been initiated since the Gulf War in 1991. The Gulf War led to the mobilization of aid for political and military purposes. As its history is important to understand today's ODA for politically unstable countries, it is pertinent to investigate the role the war played on the current topic. The war erupted in 1992. At the request of the U.S. and its allies, Japan contributed the highest amount in terms of financial support of any country (13 billion U.S. dollars). When the war ended, the government of the liberalized Kuwait issued a statement in which it expressed its thanks for the support from the U.S. and its allies. What struck the Japanese government was that the statement did not refer to Japan. Japan had provided financial support but was unable to provide military support because of the limitations of its Constitution.

Neither Kuwait nor the allies appreciated Japan's financial assistance. At the time when Japan was the leader of aid, the Japanese economy was booming. Japan was even criticized for its reliance on "cash diplomacy." Rather, the public around the world criticized Japan saying that the country did not work with "sweat and tears" on the ground.

The government took swift action to expedite members of Self-Defense Forces (SDF) abroad against strong opposition within Japan. This shocking event propelled the government to amend its rule and policy against domestic opposition in 1992. After sending military personnel to the Persian Gulf in 1991, formal PKO operations began in Cambodia and Mozambique.[9]

Though the Koizumi regime (2001–2006) will be analyzed in Chapter 4, the Iraq War, which the administration supported, was another turning point. This move responded to initiatives taken by the U.S. and the U.K. to assist further in politically fragile states just after the wars in Afghanistan and Iraq. The initiatives were strongly promoted by Prime Minister Blair of the U.K. and President George W. Bush of the U.S. Loans of BWIs were also provided to Iraq and other countries in the same situation. As Table 2-7 shows, Japan also provided Iraq with substantial amounts of ODA in cooperation with the U.S. and the U.K.

As a global partner, Japan has expanded its ODA from countries with economic needs to those with political and military problems. Though its increasing presence is not large, its direction has led to worsening relationships with its neighbor, China.

(3) Administrative Structures

There is no law pertaining to economic cooperation and aid in Japan. The incumbent governments have planned these policies in collaboration with the bureaucracy. ODA Charters were agreed on at cabinet meetings and not formally discussed in the parliament.

More than 10 ministries and agencies were involved in aid activities. Bureaucrats of the Foreign Ministry and of the ministry in charge of commerce and industry were powerful in terms of bilateral cooperation endeavors, while the Ministry of Finance was at the helm for the purposes of representing the country in multilateral cooperation efforts. But loans, and OOF in particular, were decided jointly with the ministries in charge of commerce, industry, and finance.

For a long time, the MOFA was the prime organization for foreign aid. While MOFA was in charge of bilateral aid, the Ministry of Finance was

---

[9]At that time, there was strong opposition to the deployment of officers of Self-Defense Forces (SDF). During this period, they resigned temporarily from the SDF and joined the PKO operations. There were many strong constraints against the participation of the SDF. After World War II, Japan has not had any army, only an SDF, which is an army for self defense.

responsible for provision of funds to the IMF and the World Bank. The United Nations-related issues are handled by MOFA. As explained in Section 2.1.2, financial loans of ODA were taken by the four governmental institutions already mentioned.

In 2001, a new governmental apparatus started with mergers of ministries and agencies. MOFA was accorded strong leadership for economic cooperation and aid. It used to be said that there was no coordination among ministries and agencies involved in economic cooperation and aid. The phenomena may continue to this day.[10]

However, a central planning organ at the political level composed of key ministers was created in the government for strategies of economic cooperation and aid during the Koizumi administration between 2001 and 2006. This move was to take leadership by government and not politicians, which had been supported by strong bureaucrats with budgetary allocation powers since the end of World War II. Even the budget preparations and implementations were handed over to government ministers, not those of the strong Ministry of Finance.

Prime Minister Abe took over the system. The mechanism is called the Council on Economic and Fiscal Policy. This means that activities and projects of economic cooperation and aid are coordinated and integrated if necessary and that cooperation and aid are more closely linked to national goals like poverty reduction in low-income countries and budget constraints.

2.3 Implications for China's Aid

The characteristics of Japan's aid to Africa in relation to those of China's are presented as follows:

(1) As a late-comer in terms of provision of ODA, Japan has tried to pursue its own aid policies. While Asia was a priority region, Africa was regarded as a source of mineral and energy resources. It also relied on

---

[10] Asked by the author about coordination among aid budgets, a manager of MOFA told the author that he could not say anything about the budget of aid sections of other ministries like the Ministry of Industry, formerly MITI.

financial assistance, and based on its own economic success, economic infrastructure and production sectors were priorities.
(2) The philosophy of the ODA Charter was to support self-help efforts. It is true that aid was linked to trade and investment in Asia but not in Africa. Africa was not important for economic reasons but for political and other reasons.
(3) After the 1980s, the country was obliged to adopt the measures of aid reforms led by European donors. Japan had to write off its enormous debt, which was owed by countries in Africa, and had to follow aid coordination. As a member of G7 and of DAC countries, Japan could pursue its own ODA policies within the overall aid coordination context set by the Europeans. Thus, ODA was geared to social sectors in Africa.
(4) As a global partner for global issues like poverty reduction, MDGs, and SDGs, Japan naturally paid much attention to SSA. This move was also strengthened with Japan's involvement in countries that are in unstable political and military situations.
(5) Japan's development banks were privatized in the country's overall financial reforms. They cannot take on very risky projects, which could be the case in Africa. China has not had such reforms and can provide large amounts of loans because they are backed by the central government. In the next chapter about China, one can see how large loans by the China EXIM function.

Chapter 3

Aid to Sub-Saharan Africa by China

In this chapter, China's aid to Africa will be summarized. Emphasis will be placed on increase in aid based on substantial growth of economic relations and its strong commitment, but different from Western approach (which is called "Beijing Consensus"). As in Chapter 2 about Japan, the author pays attention to differences between Western and Chinese approaches to aid, the latter being an emerging donor in this domain. This is because China referred to these differences and those with Japan. Also presented are results about the author's interviews with Chinese and French scholars and experts in their respective countries.

Section 3.1 will deal with performance of aid to developing countries in general terms as well as in terms specific to the SSA. Trends and achievements of aid will be analyzed with substantive data until the early 21st century. In Section 3.2, the same will be analyzed for the period until today.

3.1 From Tazara Railway to Major Economic Partner

Taking the same approach as in Chapter 2, China's performance with respect to aid will be analyzed in Section 3.1.1 in the context of the overall economy, international economic relations, and economic cooperation, which corresponds to aid or ODA. Policies for the overall economy and economic relations will also be discussed. Section 3.1.2 will deal with those for economic cooperation.

3.1.1 *Surge of Economic Powers since the 1980s*

(1) Overall Economic Trends

In this part, developments in macroeconomy will be summarized. GDP and its components will be dealt with. China started to open its economy in 1979 and accelerated its momentum after 1992. Growth rates since then were spectacular: 10.5 percent as an average annual growth rate from 1991 to 2000, another 10.5 percent from 2001 to 2010 (see Table 2-1 in Chapter 2). To look at GDP components, industrial sectors especially manufacturing contributed to the high economic growth.

On the expenditure side, the spectacular growth was based on substantial increase in exports and investments (see 3.1.1(2)). The foreign earnings earned by exports were the basis for the growth and development of the country. As will be explained in the next part 3.1.1(2) below, China's foreign investment from abroad started to increase significantly during the 2000s. After entry in the WTO in December 2001, many foreign enterprises of Western nations including Japanese ones also came to China for the huge domestic market. Its high growth required substantial mineral and agricultural resources from abroad. As one source, Africa became important for the second-largest economy in the world.

As explained in Section 2.1.1 about Japan, China surpassed Germany in nominal GDP in 2006 and Japan in 2010. Even its real GDP became larger than U.S. in 2015.[1] It also became the world's largest exporter, replacing Germany in 2006 and toppled Japan in 2010 to become the largest holder of foreign reserves. In comparison with Japan as explained in Chapter 2, China followed Japan's development path, hosting the Olympic Games in Beijing in 2008 and International Exposition (EXPO) in Shanghai in 2010. It was about 40 years later, namely Tokyo Olympic Games in 1964 and Osaka EXPO in 1970. Japan's "bullet" trains introduced in 1964 for the Olympic Games were followed by China's rapid trains in 2008. Techniques initially introduced by Japanese and German companies were assimilated within China so that the latter developed its own industry for manufacturing trains and the relevant systems. China and Japan are now competing for exports.[2]

---

[1] IMF, Statistical Appendix, *World Economic Outlook April 2016*.
[2] In May, 2017, the author took a linear motor train to the city of Shanghai from Pudon International Airport. The maximum speed of 431 km/h is recorded as the fastest in the Guinness World Records.

Another example for China's follow-up of Japan's experiences was a bilateral talk with the U.S. As China had started a strategic and economic talk on a bilateral basis with the U.S. in 2005, it demonstrated its success in development in the world. In fact, the U.S. regarded China as a main partner for economic and political affairs. While Japan had the Structural Impediments Initiative Talks with the U.S. starting in late 1980s, the talks concentrated on economic issues as Japan had been relying on American military for its defense.

This aforementioned 40-year or equivalent time difference is important to understand and analyze aid interventions by Japan and China in the following ways:

(1) China caught up with Japan in a remarkably short period. China has become a rival on the economic front. For example, the country and Japan are now competing in exports of their train systems to other countries, both developing and developed, which include the U.K. This contest will be discussed further in Chapter 5.

(2) There are some areas where Japan still has a technical advantage. For example, some of these areas are in environmental conservation and efficient management of infrastructures. Though China graduated from a main recipient of Japan's aid, the former appreciates the latter's technical edges in those fields. This is true for Chinese industries which depend on high-tech products from Japan.

(3) Japan is now regarded as a developed country, being a member of G7 and of DAC of OECD. China still regards itself as a developing country, taking sides with other developing countries. As explained in Chapters 1 and 2, Japan was forced to follow aid reforms led by Western donors since the 1980s. On the other hand, China is not obliged to follow suit. China itself established the Asian Infrastructure Investment Bank (AIIB) and a BRICS development bank together with other BRICS countries (Brazil, Russia, India, China and South Africa). This was regarded as a challenge to the BWIs and Asian Development Bank established by Japan with Western donors.

(4) Japan also attends the Asian–African or Afro–Asian Conference (Bandung Conference). It pays attention to South–South Cooperation just the same way as China. That is why Japan is active in promoting third country training. It has designated many countries as places for

the training mainly supported with Japan's financial assistance and partly assisted with dispatches of Japanese technical assistance experts.

To sum up, because of tremendous development since the 1980s, China's foreign reserves increased significantly. Those foreign earnings made China start to invest abroad. As will be explained later, China's foreign investment abroad increased significantly during the mid-2000s. In addition, foreign aid could increase based on this successful development. This development is written in the white paper on foreign aid first published by the Government of China in 2011 as follows: "In the 21st century, especially since 2004, on the basis of sustained and rapid economic growth and enhanced overall national strength, China's financial resource for foreign aid has increased rapidly, averaging 29.4% from 2004 to 2009."[3] The increase in foreign investment abroad and in foreign aid coincided with each other.

(2) International Economic Relations

Taking the same approach as in Chapter 2 about Japan, international economic relations will be analyzed from external trade to investment. This analysis corresponds to major items of the balance of payments tables. As China restricted portfolio investment, it will not be dealt with in this book. The following analysis uses mainly data on the Direction of Trade Statistics of the IMF and the *World Investment Report (WIR) of the UNCTAD*.

(a) External Trade

As regards to exports, growth rates of exports were high, sustaining GDP and investment. The 1990s saw an opening up of coastal areas around Shanghai in addition to zones in the south of the country. In these areas, there created special export zones which attracted massive investment from abroad, many from Japan. After China's entry in the WTO in December 2001, the Chinese Government opened the domestic markets to overseas traders and investors. Substantial inflows especially from Japan happened to invest for the huge domestic market. Many of Japanese companies also came from regions around Japan. Since that time, Chinese

---

[3] Xinhua Net, http://news.xinhuanet.com/english2010/china/2011-04/21/c_13839683_3.htm (May 17, 2017).

enterprises could develop itself in competition with overseas traders and investors. This was another important foundation for its own outward investment and exports.

China's shares of exports in the world increased substantially. Asia, Japan, and the U.S. were important destinations for China's exports. Africa's shares in China's total exports were not high. According to the External Trade Statistics of IMF, shares of exports to Africa including North Africa in China's total exports to the world were less than 1.5 percent for all years from 1991 to 1997. Those for SSA increased slightly to 1.7 percent in 2004, 1.6 percent in 2005, and 2.6 percent in 2010.

But China's presence in exports is very high for African economies. Table 2-2 in Chapter 2 shows relationships of exports for major economies with Africa. As major findings from the table, it could be understood that African countries export sizable amounts of fuel and mineral products to China. For Japan, Table 2-2 shows that its shares are small compared to those of China and U.S.

Concerning imports, China continuously increased them to support GDP and investment. But the Chinese government took measures to contain the imports so that foreign shortages could not become bottlenecks to growth and development of the economy.

The shares of the imports also grew significantly in the world. According to Table 2-2, China's shares in imports by Africa were larger than the exports. High growth rates of African economies certainly needed imports from China. China is the world's second-largest importer of petrol after the U.S. It is reported that that was why the country invested in African oil producing countries like Sudan and Angola.

Shares of imports from Africa including North Africa in China's total imports were less than 2.0 percent for all years from 1991 to 1997. Those for SSA were 2.4 percent in 2004, 2.5 percent in 2005, and 3.5 percent in 2010. Japan's shares with Africa were slightly smaller (see Section 2.1.1). But China relied on imports of materials and energy from abroad and resorted to SSA as an alternative source (see Table 2-2 in Section 2.1.1 and Table 3-1).

It is important to note that for external trade of China, exports always surpassed imports. This trade balance in surplus was a basis for China's development as well as Japan's.

Table 3-1 China's Relationships with Africa

		Rights of Petrol Exploration	Number of Chinese Kernen & Vulliet (2009)	
			Number	Year
North Africa				
1	Algeria	○	8,000	2003
2	Egypt	○		
	other three countries (Libya, Morocco, Tunisia)			
Sub-Saharan Africa				
1	Angola	○		
2	Benin			
3	Burkina Faso	○		
4	Burundi			
5	Cameroon	○	1,000~3,000	2005
6	Central African Republic			
7	Cabo Verde			
8	Chad			
9	Côte d'Ivoire		1,000	2002
10	Republic of Congo	○		
11	Democratic Republic of the Congo			
12	Djibouti			
13	Equatorial Guinea	○		
14	Ethiopia	○	2,000	2004
15	Gabon	○		
16	The Gambia	○		
17	Ghana		6,000	2004
18	Guinea			
19	Guinea-Bissau			
20	Kenya			
21	Lesotho		5,000	2005
22	Liberia		600	2006
23	Madagascar			
24	Malawi			

(*Continued*)

Table 3-1 (*Continued*)

		Rights of Petrol Exploration	Number of Chinese Kernen & Vulliet (2009)	
			Number	Year
25	Mali			
26	Mauritania			
27	Mauritius		30,000	2005
28	Mozambique		1,500	2006
29	Niger			
30	Nigeria		50,000	2005
31	Rwanda			
32	São Tomé and Príncipe			
33	Senegal			
34	Sierra Leone			
35	Somalia	○		
36	Republic of South Africa		100,000~	2004~2005
37	Sudan		5,000~10,000	2004~2005
38	Tanzania			
39	Togo			
40	Uganda			
41	Zambia			
42	Zimbabwe		10,000	2005
	other six countries (Botswana, Gambia, Namibia, Seychelles, South Sudan, Swaziland)			
	Total		220,000~427,000	

Sources: Kernen, A., & B. Vulliet, "Petits commerçants et entrepreneurs chinois au Mali et au Sénégal," *Afrique contemporaine, Agence française de développement, 2008-4*, numero 228.
Yomiuri Daily Newspaper, September 15, 2010.

(b) Foreign Direct Investment (FDI)

FDI inflow to China will be discussed first, followed by outflow, say China's investment abroad. The latter is related to aid to Africa. According to data of the International Financial Statistics (IFS) of the IMF, it should be noted that it increased substantially in mid-2000s. There were jumps in values during the period. In addition, the *WIR of the UNCTAD* has data on investment and capital stock. The inflows grew at the same pace of the above statistics of the IMF.

With respect to policies for inward investment from abroad, the State Council (Government) announced new regulations on overseas investment in April 2010, promoting good business conditions but restricting funds to environmentally unsound projects.

Concerning outflows of FDI, Table 2-3 in Chapter 2 shows that the outflows increased significantly from 2005, more substantially from 2008. Its level surpassed that of Japan in 2015. According to the WIR 2016, China was investing more than 100 billion U.S. dollars for the fifth consecutive year. There were measures taken for outward investment in mid-2000s.

Regarding its geographical distribution, *China Yearbook 2011* published by the Chinese Government uses ODI as an outflow. Its shares of accumulated total of overseas development investment (ODI) or outward investment was 75.5 percent to Asia and 12.5 percent to Latin America by 2009.[4] Eighty percent of ODI in 2011 went to developing countries.[5] Africa's share was not high.

Developing toward higher stages, China's investment abroad drew much attention. Its purchase of PC sections from IBM by Lenovo in 2005 was evidence of China's power. Since December 2001, moreover, major investments have been geared toward advanced economies. For example, three of four investments in German enterprises were made by regional enterprises of China in 2014. This latest development means that China is competing for high technology goods with Japan and Western countries.

(c) Relationships with Africa

Table 2-2 has already shown significant dependence of African economies on China. Though the shares of imports and exports were small for China, they were substantial for many African countries. In more detail, using the same Direction of External Trade Statistics, China has close relationships

---

[4] Department of Information Services, *China Yearbook 2011*, p. 498.
[5] Department of Information Services, *China Yearbook 2012*, p. 500.

with resource rich countries in Africa. To look at external trade on a country basis for 2013–2014 (the same as Table 2-2), half of exports from Angola and the Republic of Congo, fuel exporters, went to China. China's shares in total for Ethiopia, Ghana and Tanzania were 10 to 15 percent respectively. Regarding imports from China, a quarter of imports were for Ghana and Tanzania, and 15 percent for Ethiopia and Kenya. Forty per cent of Angola's imports came from China. As shown from the statistics, Angola depends too much on China for both exports and imports.

Based on "Overseas Direct Investment by Countries or Regions," published in China's *Statistical Yearbook* by the Ministry of Commerce, the following were major destinations of China's outward investment in 2004: Republic of South Africa (RSA) 10th, Guinea 14th, Nigeria 17th, Japan 18th. In 2015, Guinea, Madagascar, Nigeria, South Africa, and Sudan were major partners for investment.[6]

The author made a survey of the White Papers on Trade and FDI in Japanese published by Japan External Trade Organization (JETRO). The time period in question was from 2003 to 2014. It was understood that Sudan recorded 146.7 million U.S. dollars as an investment from China in 2004. The country ranked fourth after Cayman Islands, Hong Kong and Virgin Islands, but before the U.S. and Australia.[7] Sudan was the 10th-largest recipient of China's investment in 2005.[8]

There are large African markets in China. Provinces were accorded by the central government to encourage their own investment abroad. Some regions have large markets linked to African markets. The coastal regions especially the southern part have had markets connected to African markets.

In more detail, *China Yearbook 2013* reports that there are more than 2,000 companies for non-financial investment abroad.[9] The same order of the number of Chinese companies is also cited in other publications like

---

[6] National Bureau of Statistics, *Statistical Yearbook 2016*, p. 378.
[7] Japan External Trade Organization (JETRO), *Annual Report on World Trade and Investment 2007* (in Japanese), p. 166.
[8] In 2010, major projects for uranium in Niger received 53 million U.S. dollars and for iron core in Guinea, 1.35 billion U.S. dollars, from China as investment.
[9] Department of Information Services, *The Republic of China Yearbook 2016*.

IMF's.[10] China also takes many laborers abroad for investment. Its *Statistical Yearbook* records data on labor services for many countries around the world. It is frequently reported that there are many Chinese on the African continent: on the lower side, 1 million people. Other sources may cite 2 or 3 million Chinese in Africa (see Table 3-1). On a country basis, the data on laborers in overseas contracts will not separate official aid from private investment because they are made public in packages of those economic assistance to Africa.

To sum up for trade and investment, increase in exports earned China foreign reserves for investment as well as foreign aid. At the same time, exports required markets abroad. It should also be noted that high growth of Chinese economy needed to import from abroad. Africa's shares in exports and investment in China's totals were small. But Africa's relationships with China were substantial for many African countries, especially resource rich countries.

(3) Economic Cooperation and Aid

As in Chapter 2 on Japan, economic cooperation will be analyzed holistically. First, economic cooperation as a whole will be explained, followed by its components, namely those corresponding to ODA and OOF.

(a) Economic Cooperation

Japan and other DAC countries present data on economic cooperation, using the same definitions and compositions. The economic cooperation is composed of ODA, OOF, private funds and non-profit funds by NGOs. The last two are private cooperation. Table A in Introduction of this book shows Japan's economic cooperation or resource flows to developing countries. Those kinds of tables are always published in the *Development Co-operation Report* of OECD and Japan's *ODA White Paper*.

When one thinks about China's aid, what is important is its composition. Both China and Japan have provided African countries with packages of aid or cooperation like ODA, OOF and private investment by private

---

[10] Chen W. et al., "Investment Renaissance," *Finance & Development (IMF)*, December 2015, Vol. 52, No. 4. JETRO reports 2,000 enterprises at the end of 2009 in its *Annual Report on World Trade and Investment 2011* (in Japanese), p. 188.

enterprises. There are no comparable data on ODA and OOF for China because China is not a member of OECD/DAC. But the author tries to use data published by Chinese authorities, following this ODA composition. This is the exercise by DAC of OECD in its publication on China's aid, too.

The author has made a number of surveys about economic cooperation and aid for many developing countries around the world from Nigeria to Brazil. Visiting Thailand and the Philippines about 10 times, one could enter libraries of governmental offices without any formal letter. The picture is totally different in China. Though the author tried to enter the Ministries of Foreign Affairs and of the Commerce in Beijing, the said author could not enter them. Speaking to a Japanese-speaking officer from a lobby of the Foreign Ministry, the author was refused to go and see the officer. The author was told by the officer over the phone that the only available information was that on its website.

The most powerful ministry of economic cooperation, the Ministry of Commerce, has a very big building along a road leading to Tiananmen Square. The author was even denied to enter the premise of the Ministry. Using a Chinese national to enter public offices including statistical offices in Shanghai, the author tried to interview or get information directly from them, but even the Chinese was not allowed to enter at all.

Utilizing some comparable data on China's activities, foreign aid or official aid corresponding to ODA and OOF in DAC definitions will be dealt with in the next parts (b) and (c) in this section respectively. Going back to four compositions of the DAC Report, as regards to private cooperation, private funds are investment by enterprises which are explained in the earlier part about international economic relations for China.

Non-profit funds by NGOs are not important for China. It seems that the voluntary work is not encouraged by the Government. The author has not found any report or data on them from the website of the World Bank. In Beijing, the author found a small office about NGO activities attached to a university in 2010. The officer in charge was a teaching staff member of the university. The author tried to make an appointment with him for a meeting, but in vain.

There are Chinese volunteers sent to Africa. When the author had a meeting with a professor of a national research institute in Beijing in 2010, he told the author that the Government of China would be introducing a dispatch of young people to developing countries as volunteers. The author then found in China's newspapers young female volunteers posing at local sites like a market in Africa. Japan had introduced Japanese Overseas Cooperation Volunteer (JOCV) in 1971. It was reported that the program followed that of Peace Corps of the U.S. SSA is the region which receives the largest number of JOCVs (see case study on Malawi in Chapter 6).

As regards to trends of the components of economic cooperation, according to the *DAC Report 2007*, at the United Nations high-level meeting on the MDGs on September 25, 2008, Hu Jintao, Head of State of China, declared that China had provided 27.1 billion U.S. dollars in development assistance since 1950, including 11.9 grants. The amounts which he cited could be official aid. But they might include high-interest rate loans by official banks which might be included in ODA, OOF and in private funds. There are not much data on their loans. This issue will be discussed further later in (b) and (c) in this section.

With respect to relationships with the economy and international transactions, exports have increased continuously since 1980s. Another expenditure item, investment also contributed to high economic growth. In parallel with those economic transactions, aid or economic cooperation also grew from the second half of 2000s (details in (b) in this section). Aid was one of the important packages for encouraging exports and investment.

Regarding relationships with Africa, Africa's shares in exports and investment in China's totals were small. But economic relationships with China, external trade and investment were substantial for many African countries, especially resource-rich countries. Then, aid was given accordingly.

(b) Official Development Assistance (ODA) and "ODA-like"

(i) Introduction
Regarding the data on ODA and OOF, first, unlike Japan, there are not any comparable data on the cooperation and aid for China. The author uses data and analyses about China published by the DAC of OECD. The document is the *Development Co-operation Report (DCR)*. DAC is a forum on cooperation and aid, which is composed of 30 advanced economies. Most of them are European and American donors. Japan and South Korea are also members.

Table 3-2 Estimates of Concessional Finance for Development (ODA-like Flows) of Key Providers of Development

Country	2010	2011	2012	2013	2014
Brazil	500	n.a.	n.a.	n.a.	n.a.
Chile	16	24	38	44	49
China	2,564	2,785	3,123	2,997	3,401
Colombia	15	22	27	42	45
Costa Rica	n.a.	n.a.	n.a.	21	24
India	708	794	1,077	1,223	1,398
Indonesia	10	16	26	49	56
Mexico	n.a.	99	203	529	n.a.
Qatar	334	733	543	1,344	n.a.
South Africa	154	229	191	191	148

Note: Unit of amounts is million U.S. dollars.
Source: OECD, *Development Co-operation Report 2015*.

OECD *DCR* started publishing information on non-DAC countries and areas recently. OECD staff use data coming from China. Initially, OECD used an estimate made by Chinese researchers. Then, it uses data published by Chinese authorities. The *Finance Yearbook of the Government of China* has the data on China's concessional aid. Table 3-2 shows how large China's aid was.

This aid corresponds to ODA, not OOF. It should be noted that DAC uses "ODA-like," not ODA. Because it is unknown that Chinese authorities use the same definitions as DAC. So in this book, the author also uses ODA for Japan and "ODA-like" for China. Similarly, OOF and "OOF-like." OOF will be discussed in the following part (c) "OOF and OOF-like".

(ii) Size of ODA-like

For 2008, the lowest amount of China's "ODA-like" was estimated to be 1.8 billion U.S. dollars in *DCR*. The data are based on the *Financial Yearbook of the Government of China*. The highest estimate in 2008 was 3 billion U.S. dollars. This is an estimate of Deborah Brautigam's publication, *The Dragon's Gift*.[11] She made an estimate of concessional loans by

---

[11] Brautigam, D., *The Dragon's Gift: The Real Story of China in Africa*, Oxford University Press, 2009.

EXIM Bank. The difference between the above two figures is concessional loans by EXIM. But it can be guessed that EXIM activities may include export credit and high-interest loans which may fall under OOF. The data are not available. EXIM activities will be discussed in (iv) in this section.

Using the *Finance Yearbook of the Government of China*, the author prepared Table 2-6 on China's aid from 2004 to 2014 for comparison. In the "Government Finance Section" of the *Finance Yearbook*, the data are given in heading "Foreign Affairs." As a sub-heading, there is "external assistance." This can be official aid by the Government of China. It is understood that *DCR* uses exactly the same data in its tables.

The relationship between the Foreign Ministry and other ministries, especially the Ministry of Commerce will be discussed in detail in Section 3.2.2. Many of the budgets may be used for activities led by the Ministry of Commerce. In addition, embassies and consulates in recipient countries take important responsibilities for aid (see Section 3.2.2). The budget of "external assistance" puts together budgets of aid for all the ministries and agencies concerned. It can be guessed that embassies and consulates may have staff sent by HQs of the Foreign Ministry and of the Ministry of Commerce.

Apart from Brautigram's estimate of EXIM loans for ODA, what is important is that this figure under the Foreign Ministry corresponds to bilateral aid governed by the central government. Indeed, there is an item name "multilateral organizations" in parallel with "external finance" under the same Foreign Ministry's category.

So "ODA-like" as bilateral aid is estimated to be 1.8 billion U.S. dollars in 2008 as written in *DCR*. To look at trends of aid in Table 2-6, "bilateral ODA-like" increased significantly from 2004 to 2014. The trend from 2010 will be discussed in Section 3.2.1, based also on the second white paper which deals mainly with data from 2010 to 2012.

Up until today, there has been continuous increase in "bilateral ODA-like." It should be noted here that this increase in aid or "ODA-like" corresponds to increases in investment abroad. What should be noted is that the values of the Chinese Government were gross values or expenditures, not net expenditures. Many of aid values of Japan and other donors in *DRC* are net values (see Table A in Introduction of this book).

(iii) First White Paper on Foreign Aid in 2011

This white paper was published by the State Council (Government) of China in 2011. The first paper presents some detailed data on aid in 2009. The second white paper was published in 2014. This latest information will be dealt with in Section 3.2.1.

Regarding the value of aid or "ODA-like," the figure corresponds to the one in *DCR* and the *Finance Yearbook of the Government of China*. The first white paper explains components of China's aid as follows: "China's grants and interest-free loans come from state finances, said the report, while concessional loans are raised on the market by the Export-Import Bank of China."[12] The state funds mean the above expenditure as an external assistance in the *Financial Yearbook*. It can be understood that the figure from the budget is that of bilateral aid. China EXIM (Bank) is excluded.

(iv) China EXIM Loans

As explained earlier, China EXIM's activities should be examined when one discusses ODA or "ODA-like." China EXIM, a relatively new development bank, was established in 1994. It provides export credit, low interest loans and high interest loans. Japan had an EXIM, then was merged to JBIC in 1999.

What should be checked is whether EXIM's concessional loans are loans at low interest rates which can be categorized as ODA loans. The bank's information is difficult to obtain. But the white paper in 2011 explains about concessional loans as follows:

"Concessional loans are mainly used to help recipient countries to undertake productive projects generating both economic and social benefits and large and medium-sized infrastructure projects, or to provide complete plant, mechanical and electrical products, technical services and other materials. Concessional loans are raised by the Export-Import Bank of China on the market, and since the loan interest is lower than the benchmark interest of the People's Bank of China, the difference is made up by the State as financial subsidies. At present, the annual interest rate of

---

[12] Information Office of the State Council, *China's Foreign Aid 2011*, Beijing. http://news.xinhuanet.com/english/2010/china/2011-04/21/c_13839683.htm

China's concessional loans is between 2% and 3%, and the period of repayment is usually 15 to 20 years (including five to seven years of grace). By the end of 2009, China had provided concessional loans to 76 foreign countries, supporting 325 projects, of which 142 had been completed. Of China's concessional loans, 61% are used to help developing countries to construct transportation, communications and electricity infrastructure, and 8.9% are used to support the development of energy and resources such as oil and minerals." [13]

It is noted that the EXIM loans are given at 2–3 percent interest rates. The author could confirm this on the side of a recipient. In December 2016, the author obtained a book on China's aid to francophone Africa in Paris.[14] The authors of this book are teaching staff of African universities. Table 3-3 based on the table on Côte d'Ivoire shows that interest rates were about 2 percent.

Table 3-3 Agreement of Loans Concluded with China EXIM 2011–2013 (Côte d'Ivoire)

	Million U.S.$	Interest Rate (%)	Period of Repayment, Year	Grace Period, Year
Project of Construction of Autoroute Abidjan Grand Bassam	114.8	2.0	20	7
Project of Water Supply from Bonoua to Abidjan (Mn Yuan)	602	1.5	20	7
Project of Maintenance Hydroelectric of Soubré	500	2.0	20	9

Source: Bamba, A., "L'activisme Chinois en Côte d'Ivoire ou l'application du Principe de Non-Ingérence: 2000–2013," Mbabla, O., & Wassouni, F. (eds) *La Présence Chinoise en Afrique Francophone*, Monde Global, 2016.

---

[13] Xinhua Net, http://news.xinhuanet.com/english2010/china/2011-04/21/c_13839683_5.htm (May 17, 2017).
[14] Mbabia, O., & Wassouni, F. (eds.), *La Présence Chinoise en Afrique Francophone*, Monde Global, 2016.

In addition, there was a study on China's aid to Ghana by the Africa Economic Research Consortium (AERC) in 2008. (AERC is an institution which provides African researchers with scholarships for policy-oriented studies.) The paper was written by researchers of the University of Ghana and they surveyed China's aid to Ghana.[15] It was reported in this paper that China's aid includes public buildings including a stadium and a fire station. The interest rate is 2 percent with a grace period of five years and a repayment period of 20 years. This is a difference with Japan which did not provide aid recipients with government buildings. Even at an initial stage, Japan was not positive in aid to social sectors advocated by Western donors because it believes that it is a responsibility of government, and that providing such assistance will harm self-help efforts.

It can be concluded that some loans of China's EXIM can be included in ODA categorization. It is also understood that China EXIM provides export credit and high interest loans. This was the case of Japan EXIM. Again there are little data on those loans by China EXIM. They can be included in OOF, not ODA.

With respect to size of loans, there is a description on cumulative totals of loans in the aforementioned White Paper 2011. It is stated that "China had provided concessional loans to 76 foreign countries, supporting 325 projects, of which 142 had been completed."

What is important is that "of China's concessional loans, 61% are used to help developing countries to construct transportation, communications and electricity infrastructure, and 8.9% are used to support the development of energy and resources such as oil and minerals." It is now understood that many of EXIM loans are given to large-scale infrastructure projects. "OOF-like" will be discussed in (c) later.

---

[15] Tsikata, D. *et al.*, "China–Africa Relations: A Case Study of Ghana," A Draft Scoping Study Prepared for the African Economic Research Consortium, Institute of Statistical, Social and Economic Research, University of Ghana, January 2008, pp. 1–28. http://dspace.africaportal.org/jspui/bitstream/123456789/32068/1/Ghana.pdf?1 (May 21, 2017).

(v) Contents of ODA-like

In addition to the concessional loans or loans at some interest rates, grants and interest-free loans are also provided by China. The white paper in 2011 has the following description:

> "*Grants*
>
> *Grants are mainly used to help recipient countries to build hospitals, schools and low-cost houses, and support well-digging or water-supply projects, and other medium and small projects for social welfare. In addition, grants are used in projects in the fields of human resources development cooperation, technical cooperation, assistance in kind and emergency humanitarian aid.*
>
> *Interest-free Loans*
>
> *Interest-free loans are mainly used to help recipient countries to construct public facilities and launch projects to improve people's livelihood. The tenure of such loans is usually 20 years, including five years of use, five years of grace and ten years of repayment. Currently, interest-free loans are mainly provided to developing countries with relatively good economic conditions.*"[16]

Regarding size of those loans, the author tries to get the data from the institutions and organizations involved. It is then stated in the paper that "Unlike many of the world's top aid donors, which have dedicated development agencies — such as the UK's Department for International Development, or USAID — Chinese foreign aid projects are managed and coordinated directly by China's embassies and consulates abroad."

DAC Report cites the above activities of China's aid. Anyhow, the previously mentioned statistical data can be included as those on ODA. But there are not any data on aid published by the embassies and consulates. Referring to the aforementioned white paper again, it is stated that "China's grants and interest-free loans come from state finances." The data on the state finances are available in the *Financial Yearbook* and *Statistical Yearbook of the Government of China*. To be exact, there is an

---

[16] Xinhua Net, http://news.xinhuanet.com/english2010/china/2011-04/21/c_13839683_5.htm (May 17, 2017).

item called "external assistance." The value is spilt in state funds and provincial funds. The latter is very small.

Further analyses are needed for the funds by provincial governments. As discussed earlier, the funds are small. But FDI by provincial governments are very large. The central government has accorded rights to invest abroad to provincial governments. The author had contacts with researchers from a research institute of Tianjin City Council (provincial government) from 2009 to 2011. Through the author's interviews with several researchers and exchanging of information and opinions with them in Tianjing, it was realized that those researchers had been sent to African countries to conduct studies and that they were not familiar with DAC practices, for example, DAC five evaluation items, and its publications. It is unfortunate that the author's contacts were suddenly severed with no correspondence with those very intimate researchers since then. The research institute of Tianjin does not exist, though the author had met the Director twice.

(vi) History of Aid

To understand the aforementioned data, it is important to explain a short history of China's historical events. The white paper in 2011 presents the following history since 1950s:

> "China's foreign aid began in 1950, when it provided material assistance to the Democratic People's Republic of Korea (DPRK) and Vietnam, two neighboring countries having friendly relations with China. Following the Asian-African Conference in Bandung, Indonesia in 1955, the scope of China's aid extended from socialist countries to other developing countries, along with the improvement of China's foreign relations. In 1956, China began to aid African countries."[17]

It is realized that as a socialist country, China has had a long history for aid to Africa since 1956. Section 3.1.2 will deal with the Asian-African Conference in detail.

A symbolic project was a construction of the Tanzania–Zambia or Tazara railway, which was financed by a 500 million-U.S. dollar

---

[17] The explanation of the project is given in "Course of Development in Foreign Aid," an introductory part of "I. Foreign Aid Policy," White Paper 2011.

interest-free loan from Beijing between 1970 and 1975. The construction was needed because of a closure of transport routes in Zimbabwe where the white minority declared unilateral independence. With the construction of this new railway, Zambia could transport goods to Dar es Salaam in Tanzania without a transport route through Zimbabwe and Benguela Railway destroyed in Angola's civil war.[18]

China gave to Tanzania and Zambia no-interest loans and mobilized about 20,000 Chinese and more than 30,000 local laborers. The railway was handed over to the two governments on July 14, 1976.[19]

This project has the following significant facts as a historical background:

(1) China was allowed to belong to the United Nations in 1971. Taiwan was expelled. Since then, China campaigned to persuade African countries and other developing countries to recognize the government of People's Republic of China in Beijing. This railway was a symbolic project by China for a leading country in SSA.
(2) The project was given when China had a period of the Cultural Revolution or red army purge from 1966 to 1976. It seems that despite the political and economic turmoil, there was a strong diplomatic commitment which made this project proceed.
(3) Referring to the second white paper in 2014 and other related statements by top Chinese officials, this is the only large-scale project. It was symbolic. There were not many other projects in large size. It means that China's aid was not very large compared to aid by Western donors including Japan during the period.

---

[18] The length of the railway was 1,859 km with width of 1,067 mm.
[19] Provost, C., "China Publishes First Report on Foreign Aid Policy," *Guardian*, 28 April 2011. https://www.theguardian.com/global-development/2011/apr/28/china-foreign-aid-policy-report (May 21, 2017).
The Chinese government this week denied that its aid policy in Africa is motivated by a desire to secure natural resources. On Tuesday, the Chinese vice-commerce minister, Fu Ziying, said foreign aid to Africa was motivated by solidarity. He pointed to China's role in constructing the Tanzania-Zambia railway, which was financed by a $500m interest-free loan from Beijing between 1970 and 1975. "Just as western countries abandoned newly independent Africa, the Chinese came," said Fu. "Sixty nine sacrificed their lives and thousands labored with the Tanzanian and Zambian people. Why? For friendship."

(4) The project cost was enormous: 500 million U.S. dollar interest-free loan from Beijing between 1970 and 1975. Japan had the biggest project of all time: construction of a bridge in Congo. It cost 100 million U.S. dollars. See (vii) in this section.
(5) The project was not a success. The Tazara Railway was not a very reliable route for landlocked countries, Zambia and Malawi, even Zimbabwe and Shaba region of Congo. The author stayed as a United Nations macro-economist in Malawi from 1983 to 1987. Because of civil wars in Mozambique between the pro-Marxist government and rebel forces, the two main transport routes to Beira and Maputo were severed. Malawian bureaucrats and the author discussed various options for rerouting. Without resorting to Tazara Railway, Malawi derouted its traffic toward Durban Port in South Africa. The length to Dar es Salaam was some 1,200 km. But road and rail transport routes to the South African port were used. The distances were much more than 2,000 km. This cost Malawi 40 percent of import bills for transporting agricultural products.
(6) It is interesting to note that as discussed in Chapter 1, Tanzania was a model of aid reforms by Western countries. The Sector Investment Programs (SIPs) with Common Basket Funds were first introduced.
(7) Tanzania was regarded as important by Chinese authority (the author will discuss this in Chapter 5). The current General Secretary, Xi, was elected in November 2012. One of the first African countries visited soon was Tanzania. The country provides a sea port for China as part of the China's String of Pearls Strategy.[20]

All in all, except Tazara Railway, throughout the period until the 1990s, China's economic cooperation did not draw much attention at international scenes. The major donors for Africa were Western countries including Japan and, to a lesser extent, Soviet Union. There was a competition in aid between Western and Eastern blocs.

There are two reasons for low profiles of China's presence during the period. First, there were domestic political movements like the Cultural

---

[20] This is a maritime route for China which stretches from the Strait of Malacca to Middle East through Indian Ocean and Eastern Africa. Strings of ports in those areas look like strings of pearls.

Revolution in China. Second, there was a confrontation between Soviet Union and China.[21]

(vii) Japan's Big Project in Africa
Comparable to Tazara Railway in the 1970s was a construction of a bridge at Matadi in the People's Republic of Congo (then, Zaire) by Japan. During the period, Japan provided 100 million U.S. dollars for a construction of a Matadi Bridge over the Congo River. It was the largest project in value for Japan since its provision of ODA after World War II. Like Tazara Railway, this bridge was called a bridge of friendship for Japan and Africa. The author visited the project site in 1988 for a study on the country for an aid agency.

At that time, one of the important bottlenecks for Zaire was the transport of mineral resources from inland area of Shaba. This area was called a Copper Belt together with the other side of Zambia. The area of Shaba was one of the largest productive areas of cobalt as well as copper. The mineral resources were transported to Dar es Salaam through Tazara Railway built by China, and sea ports of Mozambique and of South Africa.

The sea ports of Mozambique were disrupted by civil wars in Mozambique. Tazara railway and Dar es Salaam port were not efficient because of a deterioration of their economies. The routes to ports of South Africa were very distant. Given this background and to encourage integration of Shaba area in the domestic economy,[22] Zairean Government tried to transport the mineral resources from the area to a port leading to the Atlantic Ocean.

Matadi and Kinshasa, capital of Zaire, had river ports on the Zairean River, now the Congo River. The project was to construct a bridge from Matadi town to the other side of the river which leads to the Atlantic Ocean. This route was also an economical route for the capital, too. Then, the EU was expected to build a modern port at Boma leading to the Ocean. The bridge is a suspension bridge that was built from 1979 until 1983. It is 722 m long with a main span of 520 m.

Because of a fall of commodity prices and the subsequent economic crisis in Zaire, the EU abandoned the project to build a sea port which should

---

[21] "Course of Development in Foreign Aid" is an introductory part of "I. Foreign Aid Policy," White Paper 2011.
[22] There had been a separatist movement in Shaba area. Monopolizing the mineral resources, some politicians of the region desired an independence.

have been linked to Matadi Bridge. The transport route from inland areas of Shaba and of Kinshasa were not established through the Matadi Bridge.[23]

(c) OOF and OOF-like

(i) China Development Bank (CDB)
It is important to discuss loans by the China Development Bank (CDB). When the author had an interview with an officer in charge of China at AFD in Paris in 2010, he mentioned that CDB should be taken into account when China's involvement in Africa is discussed. The basic data were already presented in Chapter 2. There are little data on their activities. The bank may provide many loans to provinces within China. Their loans might be high interest loans. While China's EXIM are certainly included in OOF, loans of CDB may not be. CDB is not included to discuss ODA in this book.

In case of Japan, JBIC provides export credit and loans at high interest rates. The Bank provides loans which fall in OOF. According to its journal, moreover, JBIC officials discuss possibilities of cooperation including joint lending with China EXIM and CDB for infrastructure in China and that in One Belt One Road Project, namely Silk Road Project whose maritime route stretches to Eastern Africa.[24]

(ii) China EXIM
China EXIM's low interest loans were discussed earlier and that they are included in "ODA-like." But EXIM provides export credit and high interest loans, too. They are not included in "ODA-like," but in "OOF-like."

In case of Japan, loans of Japan EXIM was not included in ODA. There was another organization called OECF which provided ODA loans. The two institutions were merged into JBIC in 1999. Then, low interest loans which had been provided by OECF were handed over to JICA. JICA, basically a technical assistance agency, started to include jobs for lending low interest loans.

As discussed in Chapter 2 for Japan, roles of OOF have become very important. This is because infrastructure projects promoted by Japan and

---

[23] In 1988, the author crossed the bridge twice. There was no car passing. The bridge was printed in the country's note (money).
[24] JBIC China Report, No. 1, 2016.

China require large amounts of money. In addition, the countries can take a free hand for OOF in the situation where ODA policies and measures were constrained by Western aid practices (already discussed in Chapter 1).

As the data on their lending are not available, the values of OOF, namely high interest loans of China EXIM and CDB will not be discussed in detail in this book. But loans of EXIM may be very large when discussing China's aid to developing countries and African countries. Then, some information will be referred to when required.

With special reference to Africa, it is important to take into account China EXIM and, possibly CDB. Whenever top officials of the Government of China announce pledges of aid, the loans of China EXIM and possibly those of CDB may be included. Those pledges will be discussed in detail in Chapters 4 and 5 which will deal with a contest in aid to Africa by Japan and China, the main theme of this book.

To sum up, though exports to Africa in total exports from China were small, they were substantial for many African countries. China's FDI to SSA increased substantially from mid-2000s. In correspondence with those private activities, bilateral "ODA-like" increased steadily. The data are presented in "external finance" in the *Finance Yearbook of the Government of China*. In addition, it is guessed that low interest loans by China EXIM, some of which loans may fall in "ODA like," may have increased accordingly. In addition, "OOF-like" which includes the other activities of China EXIM and those of CDB may have increased significantly during the second half of 2000s. More details will be discussed when the author deals with announcements of aid packages by Japan and China in Chapters 4 and 5.

3.1.2 *Commitment to South–South Cooperation*

First, political structures will be analyzed. Because political powers were very strong in China. Then, policies for economic cooperation and aid will be analyzed as systematically as in Chapter 2 on Japan.

(1) Political Structure
According to the Constitution in 1982, the state legislature is National People's Congress (NPC). As China is a one-party state, decisions of the

Communist Party reflect the policies of the country. The Politburo Standing Committee of the Central Committee of the Communist Party effectively runs the country. It consists of several mostly elderly figures. The members form China's leadership team.

In November 2002, Hu Jintao became General Secretary of the Party at a meeting of the Central Committee of the Communist Party of China. Other members were also selected, which included Wen Jiabao, an expected premier of the government. Then, the following March, Hu was elected President or Head of the State at NPC and Wen as premier of State Council which means the Government. Hu was also elected chairman of Central Military Commission in September 2004. Occupying those three important posts, Hu could supervise the Party, the State, and the Military altogether. Hu–Wen leadership continued in the second term from 2007 to 2012. They were elected just the same way as in 2002–2003.

The same process was taken for his successor, Xi Jinping. He was assisted by his premier Li Keqiang. Xi had become one of the members of the Politburo Standing Committee of the Central Committee of the Communist Party for the first time in 2007. He became General Secretary five years later. Hu and Li came from the Communist Youth League, while it is said that Xi and Hu's predecessor, Jiang Zemin, belonged to a Shanghai group.

Looking at a list of countries visited by top officials in 2016, Africa was not a priority for them. Only Egypt was visited by Xi, not country of SSA.[25]

(2) Policies for Aid

Regarding the diplomacy related to Africa, China resumed its legal seat in the United Nations in 1971, then campaigned to these countries to replace Taiwan in each of them. It established relations of economic and technical cooperation with the countries. It funded the Tazara (Tanzania–Zambia) Railway in the 1970s and other major infrastructure projects.

---

[25] Beijing Review, "Championing Positive Change," December 22, 2016, p.23. The countries President Xi Jinping visited in 2016 were Cambodia, Bangladesh and India in Asia; Iran and Saudi Arabia in Middle East; Czech Republic, Poland and Serbia in Europe; and Chile, Ecuador and Peru in Latin America. Premier Li Keqiang visited Laos, Mongolia, Kazakhstan, Uzbekistan, Latvia, Russia and Cuba. The developed countries visited were Canada and U.S.

The white paper in 2011 has the following description about foreign aid policy:

"Foreign Aid Policy
China's foreign aid policy has distinct characteristics of the times. It is suited both to China's actual conditions and the needs of the recipient countries. China has been constantly enriching, improving and developing the Eight Principles for Economic Aid and Technical Assistance to Other Countries — the guiding principles of China's foreign aid put forward in the 1960s. China is the world's largest developing country, with a large population, a poor foundation and uneven economic development. As development remains an arduous and long-standing task, China's foreign aid falls into the category of South-South cooperation and is mutual help between developing countries."[26]

As clearly given in the following statement that "China's foreign aid falls into the category of South–South cooperation and is mutual help between developing countries," as a developing country, China gives priority to South–South cooperation.

The Asian-African Conference was first held in Bandung, Indonesia in 1955. China was a leader to start this conference. Zhou Enlai led this movement with famous leaders around the world. Other prominent leaders were Jawaharlal Nehru and Sukarno. Japan has attended this conference. Prime Minister Koizumi made a statement on Japan's war against Asian countries before the opening of the summit meeting of the 50th anniversary in 2005. For the latest developments, Prime Minister Abe of Japan and General Secretary Xi of China attended 60th anniversary meeting at Bandung in 2015.

The aforementioned white paper in 2011 presents measures or policies for aid. The contents are presented in Table 3-4. To stress the importance of the eight principles announced in January 1964, the Chinese government declared in the introductory part of the white paper that the Eight Principles were the core content of which featured equality, mutual benefit and no strings attached, hence the basic principle for China's foreign aid was formulated.[27]

---

[26] Xinhua Net, http://news.xinhuanet.com/english2010/china/2011-04/21/c_13839683_4.htm (May 17, 2017).
[27] "Course of Development in Foreign Aid" is an introductory part of "I. Foreign Aid Policy," White Paper 2011.

Table 3-4 Eight Principles for Economic Aid and Technical Assistance to Other Countries (1964)

(Appendix I: China's Eight Principles for Economic Aid and Technical Assistance to Other Countries (January 1964))

1. The Chinese government always bases itself on the principle of equality and mutual benefit in providing aid to other countries. It never regards such aid as a kind of unilateral alms but as something mutual.
2. In providing aid to other countries, the Chinese government strictly respects the sovereignty of recipient countries, and never attaches any conditions or asks for any privileges.
3. China provides economic aid in the form of interest-free or low-interest loans, and extends the time limit for the repayment when necessary so as to lighten the burden on recipient countries as far as possible.
4. In providing aid to other countries, the purpose of the Chinese government is not to make recipient countries dependent on China but to help them embark step by step on the road of self-reliance and independent economic development.
5. The Chinese government does its best to help recipient countries complete projects which require less investment but yield quicker results, so that the latter may increase their income and accumulate capital.
6. The Chinese government provides the best-quality equipment and materials manufactured by China at international market prices. If the equipment and materials provided by the Chinese government are not up to the agreed specifications and quality, the Chinese government undertakes to replace them or refund the payment.
7. In giving any particular technical assistance, the Chinese government will see to it that the personnel of the recipient country fully master the technology.
8. The experts dispatched by China to help in construction in recipient countries will have the same standard of living as the experts of the recipient country. The Chinese experts are not allowed to make any special demands or enjoy any special amenities.

Source: Information Office of the State Council (People's Republic of China), *White Paper on China's Foreign Aid (Full Text: China's Foreign Aid)*, April 2011. http://news.xinhuanet.com/english2010/china/2011-04/21/c_13839683_17.htm (May 28, 2017).

One noteworthy point is that Principle 4 mentions self-reliance and independent economic development. It means development not dependent on foreign countries especially Western. A most important characteristic of China's foreign aid is no imposition of condition to aid. This is what is called "Beijing Consensus" against "Washington Consensus." The "Washington Consensus" was explained in Chapter 1. This "Beijing Consensus" will be explained in Section 3.2.2.

(3) Comparison with Japan

First, it is explained earlier that China pays attention to self-reliance. In the case of Japan, as explained in Chapter 2, self-reliance is an important philosophy. It is based on its own experience, starting as a developing country and becoming a developed country with own initiatives. China has had a strong commitment to self-reliance. Since the beginning of the Asian-African Conference (Bandung Conference), China always stressed this as a developing country. China is proud to be successful with self-reliance. This philosophy was also shared by Japan which understood this principle when its developmental level was low.

Japan also pays attention to South–South cooperation in ODA. One important point is that Japan thinks that it could become a developed country in a remarkably short time because of government-led development strategies. This is an important point when structural adjustment or market-oriented approach was introduced by Western countries in early 1980s. Committing to South–South cooperation, Japan has presented an antithesis against Western donors.

With recognition that Japan could become a developed country from a developing country, Japan always proposed that it should transfer the knowhow to other developing countries including African countries. JICA has implemented many third country training projects. It has designated many countries for home of training of trainees from other countries in the same areas. In the case of SSA, the home countries have been Kenya, Senegal and South Africa. Tunisia and Egypt were also home countries for SSA countries. JICA has had programs in Brazil for training nationals of Portuguese-speaking countries in Africa like Mozambique and Angola.[28]

Moreover, "Asian Experience for Africa" had been an important project of JICA, too. This is a third country program about a connection between Asia and Africa. The organization has sent Asian experts to Africa, for example, Thai agricultural experts were sent to East African countries.

The author had participated in a large-scale program of this kind in early 2000s. First, trainees from about 10 African countries were sent to

---

[28] The author visited a project site in Senegal in 1995. JICA had established a training center for industrial technologies. Trainees from other francophone countries have been trained at this institute. In Kenya, the author had an interview with experts for a mathematical teaching project. The project was used for teachers coming from neighboring countries. The project will be explained in Chapter 6.

Japan for training. Second, they were sent to Thailand where the governmental offices and institutions provided training programs for them. These trainees were sent to Malaysia and Singapore, too. Third, dozens of Thai experts were sent to Kenya for training programs for Africans coming from neighboring countries. This program was a medium-term program which covered fields from capacity building to agricultural extension. In the next stage, the program involved Sri Lanka.

China has built several agricultural centers in Africa. It is unknown that the technical aid is used for third countries.

3.2 Champion as an Emerging Donor

3.2.1 *China's Overwhelming Presence in Africa*

As the past trend was explained in Section 3.1.1, this part presents recent trends mainly from the start of the current financial crisis in 2008.

(1) Overall Economy and International Economic Relations

(a) General Trends
Though there was a deceleration of growth rates of GDP in recent years, the growth levels were still high compared to other countries. Its current GDP is much higher than Japan's. It is also noteworthy that its real GDP surpassed that of the U.S. in 2015, becoming the largest in the world. The spectacular growth in exports continued until recently. China's economic dependence on exports has been criticized by the U.S. and other countries which requested the country to take a demand-based development. But the continuous increase in export earnings became the source for the domestic economy and its outward investment in Africa and in other countries.

As regards FDI, China as a giant emerging market economy absorbed half of the resource flows from developed economies to emerging and developing economies in 2014. At the same time, the country is the biggest exporter of goods, and a significant investor in other emerging and developing economies as well as in developed economies like the U.K.[29] With respect to outward FDI, as China has reached a point where the

---

[29] World Bank, *International Debt Statistics*, December 2015.

outflows increase substantially, its investment around the world can be projected to grow continuously, certainly more than before.

The *Annual Report 2014 on China* published by the Government of China had the following announcement based on the Ministry of Commerce: outward investments for 2014 had 6,128 projects with 102.89 billion U.S. dollars; the cumulative investment until 2014 amounted to 646.3 billion U.S. dollars which was invested in 156 countries. The difference with inward investment was 3.56 billion U.S. dollars only. Including investment through third countries, investment by relatives and re-investment, the total amounted to 140 billion U.S. dollars, making China a net exporter of capital in 2014. The IMF data also show that China became a net exporter of capital in 2015.

The outward investment by provincial governments increased substantially to 45.1 billion U.S. dollars. Its share in total was 43.8 percent. The distribution of the investment was as follows: 9.6 billion U.S. dollars from Guangdong, 5.5 billion U.S. dollars from Beijing, 4.4 billion U.S. dollars from Shandong.

According to the latest IMF projection, China's economy is projected to increase at 6–7 percent annually. The relatively high growth is sustained by investment and exports. Though shares of exports may decline because of domestic demand-oriented strategies, many analysts agree that China remains one of the biggest economies for the future to come. Huge domestic markets continue to attract foreign investment in China. China remains as a factory of manufactured goods for the world and Africa.

(b) Relationships with Africa

China relies on some of SSA countries for importing fuel and mineral resources. There have been close relationships in terms of trade and investment. In the recent trend, Africa is needed for relocation of Chinese industries as an outward investment. The author conducted an interview with a senior official of African Development Bank (AfDB) in early 2015. According to him, Ethiopia is one of the few industrializing African countries. China started to relocate its manufacturing industries in industrial estates constructed by China in Ethiopia. This is a move to increase in wage rates in China and diversify export bases in African and Middle Eastern regions.

According to the Ethiopian Ambassador in Tokyo whom the author interviewed earlier, there were investments in manufacturing sectors by investors from China, India and Turkey. It can be noted here that China started its first industrial estate in Zambia in 1997. This was a measure for exporting China-made products in the Southern part of Africa. There are also large Chinese shopping malls in South Africa. South Africa is one of the most important allies for China in Africa.

It is noteworthy for Ethiopia that China EXIM provided a loan of 475 million U.S. dollars so that Ethiopia started operating a first metro in SSA in 2014. This is foreign aid to Ethiopia, but with high interest rates. Chinese companies were certainly engaged in the construction. It can be referred to here that China constructed a twenty-storey building of the Organization of African Union (OAU) in Ethiopia's capital, Addis Ababa. This could be investment as well as foreign aid to Africa.

Summing up, despite requests for a demand-based strategy from the U.S., high growth of exports and outward investment abroad will continue so that China's presence in Africa continues to grow. The high growth of investment and exports means that China resorts to African economies as an alternative source of fuel and mineral resources. It can be noted that Africa is a region where China can invest in monumental buildings and manufacturing which contribute to Chinese enterprises. The recent development includes relocation of Chinese industries in SSA.

(2) Economic Cooperation and Aid

(a) Economic Cooperation

In the annual *Development Co-operation Report* of OECD, there are data and analyses on the 30 main DAC and several non-DAC providers of development cooperation. There are two groups of non-DAC countries: those which report to OECD–DAC and those that do not report to DAC. The former, 19 countries and areas, follows definitions of DAC's cooperation and aid. For the latter of nine countries, OECD makes estimates of their development cooperation. There are 10 non-DAC countries whose development cooperation is estimated based on their respective government budgets.

There is a table on gross concessional financing for development in 2014 for DAC and non-DAC countries (see Table A). China is ranked 17th in value. Of non-DAC countries, Saudi Arabia and the United Arab Emirates (UAE) are within top 10. Turkey is slightly higher than China. Those three countries report to DAC. Compared to Japan on China's "ODA-like" flows, Japan's value was seven times China's in 2013. It should be noted, however, that the value of Japan was a net expenditure, while China's was a gross value.

The aforementioned comparison needs some notes. There are estimates and analyses of the development cooperation by China in the *Development Co-operation Report* annually. The estimates are based on *China's Statistical Yearbook*. The data are those of bilateral aid, not multilateral aid. In addition, China's government budget does not include concessional loans of the China EXIM Bank. Little information is available on the bank.

In the DAC Report, there are estimates of the development cooperation programs of 10 bilateral providers: Brazil, Chile, China, Colombia, Costa Rica, India, Indonesia, Mexico, Qatar and South Africa. According to the 2016 issue, China's cooperation is large compared to other developing countries like India, Brazil and South Africa (see Table 3-2).

(b) DAC Report on China's Aid
In DAC's *Development Co-operation Report*, there are written reports on non-DAC countries and areas. According to the 2016 issue, China increased its funding from 2.5 billion U.S. dollars in 2010 to 3.4 billion U.S. dollars in 2014. In 2013, 93 percent of China's development cooperation was provided bilaterally.

There are descriptions about China's multilateral flows, too. According to 2015 Report, over half of the funds were channeled through the Inter-American Development Bank, the World Bank Group and the African Development Bank. But the *Development Co-operation Report 2016* states that its cooperation is primarily channeled through the United Nations (51 percent) and the African Development Bank (45 percent). Total amount of 397 million U.S. dollars was channeled through multilateral organizations.

(c) China's White Paper on Foreign Aid 2014

The white paper on foreign aid has been published twice in 2011 and in 2014. The former was explained in Section 3.1.2. There have been references of this white paper in the DAC *Co-operation Report*. The DAC *Report 2016* reports contents of the second White Paper 2014 which includes information on the overall geographical and sectoral distribution of the program between 2010 and 2012.[30] On its geographical distribution, more than half (51 percent) of China's bilateral development cooperation went to Africa. It was followed by Asia.

The DAC *Report 2016* states that "China does not have specific priority countries (aside from the Democratic People's Republic of Korea). Its grant aid is distributed more or less equally to some 120 partner countries."[31] Putting the aid together, however, Africa was a priority region.

Regarding priority sectors, the main sectors were economic infrastructure (45 percent of bilateral funds) and social and public infrastructure (28 percent of bilateral funds). As regards forms or modes, there are eight different forms of cooperation with complete projects (turn-key projects) as the major modality. China also provides humanitarian assistance. One can guess that the previously mentioned priority sectors and modes may have been applied to SSA as well. It is true that much of China's foreign aid is given to infrastructure development.

3.2.2 From "Washington Consensus" to "Beijing Consensus"

(1) Policies for Aid

(a) South–South Cooperation

(i) Introduction

To look at the latest developments, the author explains about the second white paper published in 2014. The policies explained are the same as in

---

[30] Information Office of the State Council, *China's Foreign Aid 2014*, July 2014. http://news.xinhuanet.com/english/china/2014-07/10/c_133474011.htm (May 17, 2017).
[31] DAC/OECD, *Development Cooperation Report 2016*, p. 296. http://news.xinhuanet.com/english2010/china/2011-04/21/c_13839683_5.htm

the Paper in 2011 in Section 3.1.2. First, the 2014 White Paper states a basic policy as follows:

> "*China is the world's largest developing country. In its development, it has endeavored to integrate the interests of the Chinese people with people of other countries, providing assistance to the best of its ability to other developing countries within the framework of South–South cooperation to support and help other developing countries, especially the least developed countries (LDCs), to reduce poverty and improve livelihood. China has proactively promoted international development and cooperation and played a constructive role in this aspect.*"[32]

As stated in Section 3.1.2, South–South cooperation is key. China helps other developing countries as a developing country. That is why the word cooperation is used when referring to aid.

(ii) "Beijing Consensus"
Beijing does not set conditions as stated in the Eight Principles for Economic Aid and Technical Assistance to Other Countries (see Table 3-4). In the second White Paper 2014, this principle is reiterated as:

> "*When providing foreign assistance, China adheres to the principles of not imposing any political conditions, not interfering in the internal affairs of the recipient countries and fully respecting their right to independently choosing their own paths and models of development. The basic principles China upholds in providing foreign assistance are mutual respect, equality, keeping promise, mutual benefits and win-win.*"[33]

This statement is Beijing's policy against Western conditional aid, and is always referred to in China's policy documents and in the remarks of top ranking officials. This is what is called "Beijing Consensus," different

---

[32] Information Office of the State Council, *China's Foreign Aid 2014*, July 2014. http://news.xinhuanet.com/english/china/2014-07/10/c_133474011.htm (May 17, 2017).
[33] Xinhua Net, http://news.xinhuanet.com/english/china/2014-07/10/c_133474011.htm (May 17, 2017).

from "Washington Consensus." discussed in Chapter 1.[34] The author summarizes the major characteristics as: no conditionality or no condition to aid; direct impact (emphasis on direct production sector and economic infrastructure; link with investment.

In the first white paper on foreign aid in 2011, moreover, no interference in recipient's policies is a distinct policy by China. It is against Western practices in the context of SAP since the 1980s. In addition, the paper has "I. Foreign Aid Policy." Its part, "Basic Features of China's foreign Aid Policy," is presented in Table 3-5.

Regarding "imposing no political conditions" in one of the five features, it is written that "China never uses foreign aid as a means to interfere in recipient countries' internal affairs or seek political privileges for itself." This statement is always referred to in China's policy documents and in the remarks of top-ranking officials.

This "Beijing Consensus" is against "Washington Consensus" in the form of structural adjustment led by IMF and the World Bank under the auspices of the U.S. and its Western allies. The recipient African sides have strong opposition to conditions of aid. Though they were obliged to get debt relief and fresh assistance from IMF, the World Bank, and Western bilateral donors including Japan, African politicians, bureaucrats and scholars, even civil society activists, vehemently opposed intervention in domestic affairs.

In September 2010, the author visited Beijing, Tianjin and Paris to discuss China's economic cooperation with Africa with intellectuals and officers in charge of cooperation. The Chinese counterparts belong to a national research institute and an institute of Tianjin Regional Government. A professor of the national research institute in Beijing has visited many seminars and made presentations in English. He also visited some African countries, too. The author met him several times in Tokyo and Beijing from 2005. He was confident that Africans and Europeans appreciate "Beijing Consensus." He also picked up a three-pronged approach, a link of aid with trade and investment as a lesson from Japan (see (b) in this

---

[34] The Beijing Consensus was mentioned by Joshua Cooper Ramo in his article "The Beijing Consensus" for The Foreign Policy Centre, 2004. http://fpc.org.uk/fsblob/244.pdf

Table 3-5 Basic Features of China's Foreign Aid Policy in the White Paper 2011

— Unremittingly helping recipient countries build up their self-development capacity. Practice has proved that a country's development depends mainly on its own strength. In providing foreign aid, China does its best to help recipient countries to foster local personnel and technical forces, build infrastructure, and develop and use domestic resources, so as to lay a foundation for future development and embarkation on the road of self-reliance and independent development.
— Imposing no political conditions. China upholds the Five Principles of Peaceful Coexistence, respects recipient countries' right to independently select their own path and model of development, and believes that every country should explore a development path suitable to its actual conditions. China never uses foreign aid as a means to interfere in recipient countries' internal affairs or seek political privileges for itself.
— Adhering to equality, mutual benefit and common development. China maintains that foreign aid is mutual help between developing countries, focuses on practical effects, accommodates recipient countries' interests, and strives to promote friendly bilateral relations and mutual benefit through economic and technical cooperation with other developing countries.
— Remaining realistic while striving for the best. China provides foreign aid within the reach of its abilities in accordance with its national conditions. Giving full play to its comparative advantages, China does its utmost to tailor its aid to the actual needs of recipient countries.
— Keeping pace with the times and paying attention to reform and innovation. China adapts its foreign aid to the development of both domestic and international situations, pays attention to summarizing experiences, makes innovations in the field of foreign aid, and promptly adjusts and reforms the management mechanism, so as to constantly improve its foreign aid work.

Source: Information Office of the State Council (People's Republic of China), *White Paper on China's Foreign Aid (Full Text: China's Foreign Aid)*, April 2011. http://news.xinhuanet.com/english2010/china/2011-04/21/c_13839683_4.htm (May 28, 2017).

section). The researchers of the Tianjin institute were not aware about aid practices and reforms of DAC/OECD.

(b) Three-Pronged Approach

It is said that China's aid is linked to trade and investment. As explained in Section 3.1.1, investment and exports increased substantially in the 2000s and made China a large holder of foreign reserves. With this spectacular development, China could import to sustain its high growth and use foreign exchange for outward investment. Aid budget increased accordingly.

On the other hand, high growth needed resources from abroad, e.g., petrol. This is why China resorted to resource-rich African countries, like Sudan, Angola and Nigeria for petrol and RSA for rare metal. As explained in Section 2.2.2, Japan took this approach at least at a low level of development.

(c) Tied Aid
This tied aid is a characteristic of China's aid interventions, too. Some call this a win-win aid relationship. The author interviewed with a Chinese scholar of a national research institute in 2010. The scholar had made presentations on China's aid at international conferences. He mentioned this win-win approach as indicated in the previously mentioned quotation of the White Paper 2014.

It is reported that China's aid brings its own construction companies with many laborers from China. Many of their projects may have been linked to their own companies and nationals. Peer Reviews of DAC have criticized Japan for its tied aid. But its tying status was not very high.

(d) Global Partner
As stated in Section 2.2.1 about Japan, China also tried to provide aid as a global partner. China started its Strategic Talks with the U.S. in 2009, about 20 years later than Japan. Though further exploration surveys are needed about the role of aid policies in the Talks, the two countries implemented a joint construction project in Liberia in 2010 (see Chapter 4).

China is designated as a key partner of the OECD and collaborates with the DAC through the events of the China–DAC Study Group. China took part in the DAC Senior-Level Meeting, too.

The author conducted interviews with specialists of Africa and of China in OECD in 2010. They told the author that China was not cooperative. As a signatory of the Paris Declaration, they said that China was not taking the corresponding approaches. It was the time of failure of climatic consultations in Copenhagen in 2013. During the negotiations, China was criticized because of its opposition to proposals like monitoring of each country's efforts. It should be noted, however, that China contributed to the success in Paris Declaration on climatic issues in 2015.

(e) Comparison with Japan

At present, Japan and China commit to South–South Cooperation. But it is not clear if China provides third country programs for which Japan has been active. Regarding conditional aid, Japan also has informed Western donors that it does not set harsh conditions. Rather, it prefers a consultation, not a condition.

Japan's difference with China is that like other Western countries, the Government is now obliged to publish evaluations for the general public. Transparency and accountability of aid is an important issue. This effort has been also pointed out as a recommendation for Japan's ODA in the past peer review reports on Japan's ODA.

(2) Administrative Structures

The DAC's *Development Cooperation Report 2016* has a description about China's aid system as follows:

> *"The Ministry of Commerce's Department of Foreign Assistance is at the centre of the Chinese system and manages over 90% of its bilateral funding. It is responsible for drafting the development co-operation budget and regulations, managing foreign development co-operation joint ventures; programming zero-interest loans and grants, and co-coordinating concessional loans with the China Exim Bank (the latter are not included in OECD estimates because little information is available on their objectives or financial terms)."*[35]

This structure corresponds to the explanation of the White Paper 2011. There is information on which organizations were engaged in aid. It is stated that "Unlike many of the world's top aid donors, which have dedicated development agencies — such as the UK's Department for International Development, or USAID — Chinese foreign aid projects are managed and coordinated directly by China's embassies and consulates abroad."

But it is also written in "II: Financial Resources for Foreign Aid" that:

> *"Foreign aid expenditure is part of the state expenditure, under the unified management of the Ministry of Finance in its budgets and final accounts*

---

[35] DAC/OECD, *Development Cooperation Report 2016*, p. 296

system. The Ministry of Commerce and other departments under the State Council that are responsible for the management of foreign aid handle financial resources for foreign aid in their own departments in accordance with their respective jurisdictions. Each of these departments draws up a budget for foreign aid projects every year and submits it to the Ministry of Finance for examination, and then to the State Council and the National People's Congress for approval and implementation. Each department controls and manages its own funds for foreign aid projects in its budget. The Ministry of Finance and the National Audit Office supervise and audit the implementation of foreign aid budget funds of these departments based on relevant state laws, regulations and financial rules."[36]

Based on the aforementioned documents, the central organization is the Ministry of Commerce. But there are some ministries involved in foreign aid. Direct management and coordination is of course made by local embassies and consulates in recipient countries as stated earlier.

Chinese embassies and consulates take great responsibilities for aid activities in Africa. According to the 2013 Report published in October 2012,[37] China had embassies in 44 countries. The countries which kept diplomatic ties with Taiwan were Burkina Faso, The Gambia and São Tomé and Príncipe. The countries which did not have any Chinese recognition were Somalia and Swaziland.

According to the same report, Japan had embassies only in 23 countries. There were JICA offices in 26 countries.[38] Some of the countries which did not have any Japanese embassy had JICA offices. They were Benin, Burkina Faso, Namibia, Sudan, and South Sudan. China's presence in Africa with diplomatic corps is at the same level of the U.S., U.K. and France.

When the author interviewed with a specialist in charge of China at AFD — a French aid agency — he told the author that a foreign aid

---

[36] Xinhua Net, http://news.xinhuanet.com/english2010/china/2011-04/21/c_13839683_5.htm (May 17, 2017).
[37] Routledge, *Europa World Year Book 2013*, October 2012.
[38] JICA homepage, https://www.jica.go.jp/about/structure/overseas/africa.html. (May 17, 2017).

section of the Ministry had a small number of officers. It can be guessed that this section may be in charge of planning and budget preparation. Subsequent planning and implementation with budgetary arrangements may be dealt with by other governmental ministries and agencies and embassies and consulates in recipient countries as stated in the white paper in 2011. Especially, the latter may take more responsibility for planning, budgeting and implementation directly at local levels.

In addition, roles of provincial governments should be discussed. First, foreign aid is centralized. The budget given in the *Financial Yearbook* indicates very small budgets earmarked for provinces. Second, from the author's interviews with several researchers of a research institute of Tianjin Provincial Government in Tianjing, China's shares of ODI at provincial level are a little less than 50 percent. It can be understood that those researchers are business consultants who make studies which are not in ODA. ODA budgets in DAC countries including Japan comprise hiring of experts who conduct feasibility and evaluation studies on ODA projects.

In case of Japan, the MITI, currently the Ministry of Industry, also took aid policies especially for industrializing Southeast Asian countries. The Ministry introduced various measures like support to industrial chains for Japanese enterprises operating in the region. But the prime institution for bilateral aid is the Ministry of Foreign Affairs, while multilateral aid is handled by the Ministry of Finance.

3.3 Achievements and Trends

China's exports increased continuously since the 1980s. Regarding inflows of FDI, it contributed to modernization and development of the Chinese economy. It continuously increased throughout the 1990s and in the 21st century. In the balance sheet, based on huge foreign reserves, China started to invest abroad. The ODI or outflows of FDI increased substantially from mid-2000s to this decade. By 2015, China became a net exporter of capital. In correspondence with the private activities, "ODA-like" and "OOF-like" increased significantly during the second half of 2000s.

Aid increased in parallel with investment. There was a little time lag between investment and aid. This means that aid may have been given to support investment, especially aid loans to infrastructure development. The value of aid became very high recently.

With respect to the relations with Africa, shares of exports and investment were not very high for China until recently. It should be noted, however, that they were significant for many African countries, especially resource-rich countries. According to the white paper on foreign aid in 2014, on a geographic distribution, half of aid was given to Africa in 2010–2012.

Foreign aid system is centralized with the Ministry of Commerce. But many of activities were handled by other ministries, and embassies and consulates which exist in most of African countries, comparable to the U.S. Its diplomatic presence in Africa is much larger than that of Japan.

Based on the author's surveys of literature in China and in Paris and on the interviews with Chinese scholars and experts, a formal evaluation system of foreign aid may not have been established in China. Many experts whom the author met in China did not know DAC evaluation methods.

There may have been failures in many aid projects of China just the same way as Western donors and Japan had until late 1970s. The author happened to have a talk with a researcher who had worked for a section in charge of aid in the Ministry of Commerce. As stated previously, this ministry is a central agency for bilateral aid of China. The researcher told the author that there were many problems in the Ministry's projects and that it was a common understanding among aid specialists that many projects in Africa did not go well. The remarks of this researcher corresponded to the reports made by a professor of a national research institute whom the author met in Tokyo and in Beijing from 2005 several times. He was a prominent specialist who has made many presentations at international conferences.

One example could be agricultural centers. There are 24 agricultural centers built by China in 24 countries. Some were built and managed by enterprises, not national agencies.[39] There are such centers in 13 countries.

One should note that there was a long history of reforms in the field of agricultural extension services in Africa. The author first encountered this reform in Malawi in early 1980s. The country had started to

---

[39] Bautigam, D., *Will Africa Feed China?*, Oxford University Press, 2015.

implement a structural adjustment program led by the World Bank from 1981. Two of the author's United Nations expert team for "Project: Assistance in Development Programming" for the Government belonged to the Ministry of Agriculture. The reform was to privatize the services against inefficient system services offered in big center buildings constructed by governments with many Western donors. Most of the centers were inefficient and not well maintained. So new construction of the agricultural centers by China is a reversal of the aid reforms which were in place for many years.

Chapter 4

Rivalry between Japan and China until Early 2010s

4.1 Japan's Conservative Regime and Reaction from China

This chapter presents a short history of rival relationships between Japan's aid policies set by its conservative party and China's reaction. The aid mechanisms, namely, TICAD and FOCAC, will also be explained in detail. This chapter focuses on the period from early 2000s to 2011. The current governments of the two countries which were established in late 2012 will be dealt with in Chapter 5.

4.1.1 *Conservative Party and China*

(1) Koizumi Administration and Cold War with China

(a) Powerful Koizumi Administration
Japanese politics have been basically governed by conservative parties since the end of World War II. In recent years, the Liberal Democratic Party (LDP) is a main political party whose head has been elected prime minister of the government. In the course of economic development since the end of World War II, its polling base which had rested in rural areas was eroded because of rapid urbanization and of rising consciousness about politics among rich urban dwellers. Table 4-1 shows prime ministers of Japan together with top officials of China and of other countries. LDP became weak toward mid-1990s. To win the presidential election, LDP even upheld

Table 4-1 History of Administrations

Year	British Administration	Party in Power	American Administration	Party in Power	Japanese Administration	Party in Power	Chinese Administration
1989	Thatcher	Conservative	Bush (Father)	Republican	3 PMs	LDP	Jiang Zemin
1990	Thatcher, Major	Conservative	Bush (Father)	Republican	Kaifu	LDP	Jiang Zemin
1991	Major	Conservative	Bush (Father)	Republican	Kaifu, Miyazawa	LDP	Jiang Zemin
1992	Major	Conservative	Bush (Father)	Republican	Miyazawa	LDP	Jiang Zemin
1993	Major	Conservative	Clinton	Democrat	Miyazawa, Hosokawa	LDP, opposition	Jiang Zemin
1994	Major	Conservative	Clinton	Democrat	3 PMs	Opposition, LDP	Jiang Zemin
1995	Major	Conservative	Clinton	Democrat	Murayama, Hashimoto	LDP & Socialist	Jiang Zemin
1996	Major	Conservative	Clinton	Democrat	Hashimoto	LDP & Socialist	Jiang Zemin
1997	Major, Blair	Conservative, Labor	Clinton	Democrat	Hashimoto	LDP & Socialist	Jiang Zemin
1998	Blair	Labor	Clinton	Democrat	Obuchi	LDP	Jiang Zemin
1999	Blair	Labor	Clinton	Democrat	Obuchi	LDP	Jiang Zemin
2000	Blair	Labor	Clinton	Democrat	Obuchi, other	LDP	Jiang Zemin
2001	Blair	Labor	**Bush**	Republican	**Koizumi**	LDP	Jiang Zemin
2002	Blair	Labor	**Bush**	Republican	**Koizumi**	LDP	Jiang Zemin until Nov
2003	Blair	Labor	**Bush**	Republican	**Koizumi**	LDP	Hu Jintao
2004	Blair	Labor	**Bush**	Republican	**Koizumi**	LDP	Hu Jintao
2005	Blair	Labor	**Bush**	Republican	**Koizumi**	LDP	Hu Jintao
2006	Blair	Labor	**Bush**	Republican	**Koizumi, Abe**	LDP	Hu Jintao

Year	UK	UK Party	US	US Party	Japan	Japan Party	China
2007	**Blair**, Brown	Labor	**Bush**	Republican	Abe, Fukuda	LDP	Hu Jintao
2008	Brown	Labor	**Bush**	Republican	Fukuda, Aso	LDP	Hu Jintao
2009	Brown	Labor	Obama	Democrat	Aso, Hatoyama	LDP, DP	Hu Jintao
2010	Brown, Cameron	Labor, Conservative	Obama	Democrat	Hatoyama, Kan	DP	Hu Jintao
2011	Cameron	Conservative	Obama	Democrat	Kan, Noda	DP	Hu Jintao
2012	Cameron	Conservative	Obama	Democrat	Noda, Abe	DP	Hu Jintao until Nov
2013	Cameron	Conservative	Obama	Democrat	**Abe**	LDP	**Xi Jinping**
2014	Cameron	Conservative	Obama	Democrat	**Abe**	LDP	**Xi Jinping**
2015	Cameron	Conservative	Obama	Democrat	**Abe**	LDP	**Xi Jinping**
2016	Cameron, May	Conservative	Obama	Democrat	**Abe**	LDP	**Xi Jinping**
2017	May	Conservative	Trump	Republican	**Abe**	LDP	**Xi Jinping**
2018					**Abe (expected)**		**Xi Jinping (expected)**
2019					**Abe (expected)**		**Xi Jinping (expected)**
2020					**Abe (expected)**		**Xi Jinping (expected)**
2021					**Abe (expected)**		**Xi Jinping (expected)**
2022							**Xi Jinping (expected)**

Note: American presidents are elected in December. The above table shows the following year when they are sworn in.

a top of Socialist Party as a prime minister. There was some stability in politics as his successors, Keizo Obuchi and Ryutaro Hashimoto came from the largest faction of LDP. But erosion of popularity of LDP continued.

It was Koizumi that made Japan's politics stable from 2001 to 2006, It is reported that the current politics in Japan reflects the election of Koizumi in 2001. Koizumi revolutionized the conservative party by destroying its old-fashioned regime especially fractional practices, and by promoting new generations like Abe, the current Prime Minister from December 2012.

For foreign policy, Koizumi had a very good relationship with American President George W. Bush. Since the terrorist attack in September 2001, the Bush administration took nationalistic policies from 2001 to 2008. Koizumi and Blair of the U.K. expressed strong support for Bush. Despite strong opposition to American war against Iraq by some G7 countries like France and Germany, those two leaders supported Bush. During Koizumi tenure, some forces were sent to Iraq and Afghanistan. Japan's ODA increased for those war-torn countries, supporting forces by U.S. and its allies. With limitation of the Constitution, Japanese forces helped forces of other countries behind the battlegrounds.

(b) Relationships between Koizumi Administrations and China

Relationships with China deteriorated because of Koizumi's conservative policies. He visited Yasukuni Shrine six times which resulted in strong opposition from China and South Korea as it enshrines war criminals. Hu, President of China, asked Koizumi not to go to the shrine. Wang Yi, the then Ambassador to Japan, who is currently Foreign Minister, repeatedly condemned the visit. Abe had expressed his support to Koizumi's visit to the shrine. With his own visit in December 2013 after his election in 2012, China has questioned Abe's attitude toward the historical issues in relation to World War II.

The dispute in the East China Sea islands between the two countries also continued. The Senkaku (Chinese Name: Diaoyu; English Name: Pinnacle) Islands were a major subject of the dispute. The confrontation about this territorial issue was intensified in 2012 just before establishment of the current administrations in Japan and China.

During the six-year period from 2001 in power, there was no state visit between leaders of the two countries. Koizumi and his Chinese counterparts Jiang Zemin and Hu had summit meetings only on occasions of international conferences.

(2) Chinese Counterpart
In November 2002, Hu became General Secretary of the Party at a meeting of the Central Committee of the Communist Party of China. Other elderly members were also selected who effectively governed the country. In March 2003, Hu was elected President or Head of the State at the NPC and Wen Jiabao was confirmed as Premier of the State Council which means the Government.

Hu was also elected Chairman of the Central Military Commission in September 2004. Occupying those three important posts, Hu could assume supremacy of the nation's power. Hu–Wen leadership continued in the second term from 2007 to 2012. They were elected just the same way as in 2002–2003. The same process was taken for his successor, Xi, who became General Secretary in November 2012, current top leader of China.[1]

(3) Confrontation over Historical Issues
In April 2005, there were serious demonstrations against Japan — some peaceful, some violent — in China and in other Asian countries. A governmental decision to approve school textbooks which played down Japan's actions before and during World War II triggered the protests. A bid for permanent membership of the Security Council of the United Nations was also an issue (see (4) shortly).

There were many demonstrators in Beijing, Shanghai and other cities around China. Some Japanese premises including restaurants and supermarkets were damaged. There were a series of statements of accusations between the two governments.

(4) United Nations Security Council
Japan, with its high economic profile and aid to developing countries, wished to become a permanent member of the Security Council of the

---

[1] Xi, current president of China, had become one of members of the Politburo Standing Committee of the Central Committee of the Communist Party for the first time in 2007.

United Nations. Japan's Foreign Ministry is in charge of the United Nations and took various measures. It was reported that introduction of TICAD in 1993 was a measure for this purpose. Based on its aid to Africa and active engagement in initiatives for fragile states with the U.S. and the U.K., Japan sent diplomatic missions to Africa for voting for Japan's aspirations.

Japan formed G4 with Germany, Brazil and India. Though the U.S., France and the U.K. supported Japan's desire, China strongly opposed it. It was reported that China sent missions to African countries to persuade them not to support Japan's request. Japan and the other allies even proposed that OAU selects one or two as permanent members of the Council. But there was no decision taken by OAU. In July 2005, G4 submitted a resolution to the General Assembly meeting for enlargement of members of the Security Council. But there was no vote. With slim possibilities for the approval, Japan had to turn down its move.

(5) Abe (LDP) and His Successors and China
Koizumi stepped down after two tenures stipulated by the party law. Just after the resignation of Koizumi, his preferred heir took office. He was Abe, the current Prime Minister since 2012. On September 20, 2006, Abe won an overwhelming victory over Taro Aso and Sadakazu Tanigaki to become Chairman of LDP. Taro Aso was also a favorite of Koizumi and later became Prime Minister from 2008 to 2009. He has been vice minister who supports Abe's second administration since 2012. Abe was elected with a majority of LDP at an Interim Parliamentary Session in September 2006.

Soon after his election, his first overseas visit the following month in October was to go to China and South Korea. Japan's relationships with the two neighbors had deteriorated significantly during the Koizumi era. Though there was a rioting against Japan in the preceding year (see (3) previously), Abe was greatly welcomed in China. Abe and Hu agreed a collaboration in the future.

Abe's first administration ended one year later because of his illness. In response to his visit, Premier Wen made an official visit to Japan and made a presentation in Japan's Parliament in April 2007. Prime Minister Yasuo Fukuda of LDP had paid an official visit to China in 2007 and 2008.

Hu made an official visit to Japan in May 2008. Another favorite of Koizumi, Prime Minister Fukuda had a meeting with Hu. They signed a joint statement for strategic mutual relationships.

4.1.2 *Opposition Party and China*

Strong opposition to LDP after Koizumi had stepped down in 2006 weakened the LDP. Every year saw different Prime Ministers from the LDP: Abe from 2006 to 2007, Fukuda from 2007 to 2008 and Aso from 2008 to 2009. Finally, the Democratic Party (DP) had a landslide victory over LDP in 2009. DP was a new party established in 2003. The party was a merger of some factions which had been separated from LDP and Social Democratic Party which sympathized with China.

Prime Minister Yukio Hatoyama changed foreign policy drastically.[2] His administration took a pro-China policy and put distance from the U.S. He announced that Japan would wish to make the disputed neighboring sea a sea for friendship. A hundred of DP politicians visited Beijing and shook hands with Hu. This pro-China stance displeased the U.S.

DP took drastic measures for foreign aid, too. With substantial and comprehensive reduction in government budgets, DP cut many budgets for aid which were kept as vested interests under LDP regime.

DP took office for the first time. Its leadership did not go well with opposition from LDP as well. Their measures for Tohoku Tsunami in March 2011 weakened the leadership of DP, too. The dispute in the neighboring sea between the two countries continued. It was in 2010 that a Chinese fisherman was arrested by Japanese forces in the sea. There was rioting against Japan in many cities in China.

An important event occurred in April 2012 that a former influential nationalist congressman of LDP, Shintaro Ishihara, then a mayor of Tokyo, announced that he would buy the disputed islands to justify its belonging to Japan. Despite Hu's strong protest against PM Yoshihiko Noda of DP, DP could not take any serious action against the move. After announcement of the purchase by the Government in a move to calm down the rows in July 2012 and landing on the islands by Hong Kong

---

[2] Hatoyama was a former member of LDP. His father was Prime Minister, too.

activists on August 15, riots erupted in many cities in China in September 2012, burning Japanese restaurants, shops and cars, and injuring Japanese residents in China.

With poor governance record, DP lost to LDP in a landslide loss in December 2012. Abe was sworn in as Prime Minister for his second administration and lasts until now. In the next election in 2016, LDP won another landslide victory over DP. DP has become very weak since. It is projected that the opposition side may not win against LDP until 2021 when Abe steps down after three tenures. He changed the rule for two tenures as General Secretary of LDP. Xi, President of China, may be in office until 2022.

4.2 Tokyo International Conference on African Development (TICAD) vs. Forum on China-Africa Cooperation (FOCAC)

In this section, aid mechanism for SSA of Japan and China will be explained. Latest developments of the current regimes of the two countries will be discussed in Chapter 5. Though the mechanisms include five countries in North Africa, there will be no special reference to them. Amounts of aid to those countries are included in statements of Japan and China.

4.2.1 *TICAD since 1993 and Achievements*

TICAD is a summit level meeting which invites heads of state including those in North Africa. The first meeting was held in 1993 and followed every five years until 2013. The last meeting was held in Kenya in August 2016, first time outside Japan. The interval of the meetings was shortened from five years to three years. This corresponds to FOCAC being held every three years and alternatively in China and in an African country.

Against reduction in aid to Africa by Western donors in 1980s and 1990s, Japan increased aid to Africa in addition to Asia. Whenever TICAD was held, it was reported that one purpose for introduction of TICAD was to win a permanent member seat in the Security Council of the United Nations.

As a Western donor, Japan came to co-chair TICAD meetings with representatives of the United Nations Development Programme (UNDP), United Nations, World Bank and OAU. The basic policy of TICAD V in 2013 was as follows:

— Boost the growth of Africa through trade and investment of private sector; and
— Promote "Human Security" through Japan's unique assistance.

Contributing to the growth of Africa, Abe pledged 3.2 trillion yen (equivalent to 32 billion U.S. dollars), utilizing private and public means. ODA was earmarked for approximately 1.4 trillion yen (equivalent to 14 billion U.S. dollars) in the next three years.[3] Taking into account private investment in Africa, Abe stressed importance of aid in public and private partnership.

4.2.2 FOCAC since 2000 and Achievements

The FOCAC has been held since 2000. It is a ministerial level meeting. The objectives of FOCAC are equal consultation, enhancing understanding, expanding consensus, strengthening friendship and promoting cooperation. The FOCAC dialogue and consultation mechanism is in three levels:

— the Ministerial Conference held every three years;
— the Senior Official Follow-up Meeting and Senior Official Preparatory Meeting for the Ministerial Conference held respectively in the previous year and a few days before the Ministerial Conference; and
— meetings of African diplomats in China with the Chinese Follow-up Committee held at least twice a year.[4]

---

[3] Ministry of Foreign Affairs (Japan), Japan's Assistance Package for Africa at TICADV. http://www.mofa.go.jp/files/000006375.pdf
[4] Forum on China–Africa Cooperation, FOCAC ABC, 2013/04/09. http://www.focac.org/eng/ltda/ltjj/t933522.htm

The conference was held in China and Africa, alternatively. The first, third and fifth meetings were held in Beijing. The second held in Ethiopia, fourth in Egypt and sixth in South Africa. Some of the meetings were upgraded to be summit ones. They were held in Beijing in 2006 and in Johannesburg, South Africa in December 2015. The next meeting will be held in 2018.

At the fifth FOCAC meeting in 2012, China announced an amount of 20 billion U.S. dollars of credit to African countries. The latest pledge in 2015 was 60 billion U.S. dollars. The exchanges of pledges between Japan and China in the latest conferences will be discussed in Chapter 5.

4.3 Collaboration between Two Countries

There are some efforts to collaborate between Japan and China. In this section, the past trends will be presented, followed by possibilities of collaboration between two countries in the future in Chapter 5.

4.3.1 *Collaboration with Other Countries*

(1) China
According to the DAC *Development Co-operation Report 2016*, China is starting to engage in triangular cooperation, partnering with several international organizations (e.g., the United Nations Development Programme, the United Nations Industrial Development Organization and the World Bank) and DAC members (e.g., New Zealand, the U.K. and the U.S.).[5]

The U.K. approached China actively in the past. Both countries had established annual summit and ministerial meetings in recent years. Xi made a presentation in U.K.'s Parliament on his official visit in 2015. In a report of the DFID, there was a move to collaborate in Democratic Republic of the Congo, a former Belgian colony.

Concerning the relationships with the U.S., as already explained in Chapter 3, the two countries started Annual Dialogue. The dialogue includes joint efforts to assist third countries just the same way as in the

---

[5] DAC/OECD, *Development Co-operation Report 2016*, p. 296.

Structural Impediment Initiative with Japan. One notable example of China's aid was a joint project in Liberia in 2010. Liberia is a country established by the U.S., bringing former slaves from the U.S. back to their homeland. The two countries renovated a building of a university in Liberia.

(2) Japan

Based on its development experience from a developing country to a major donor, Japan has made serious efforts to implement third country programs with many developing countries around the world. For Africa, Japan has designated Kenya, Senegal and RSA as suitable training grounds for other Africans.

Japan has been active in joint efforts with other major donors. In fact, Japan has collaborated with the U.S. in the framework of the bilateral economic dialogue as explained in Section 2.2.1. Global Issues Initiatives (GIIs) was an important example. It was in 2013 that Japan and France issued a collaboration strategy for five years. This framework includes collaboration in Africa by the two countries. Chambers of Commerce of the two countries in Africa have developed a link of information on their companies present in the continent.

In December 2016, the author interviewed in Tokyo with an official from French Ministry of Foreign Affairs. He told the author that there were significant interventions in Africa by the U.S. and China. This is one of the reasons why France approached Japan so that the two countries could establish special cooperation relationships for the future.

4.3.2 *Japan's Collaboration with China*

As regards to the collaboration between Japan and China, there has not been significant collaboration at leaders' level. But the joint statement on a strategic collaboration in 2008 was a basis for various collaboration mechanisms. The annual meeting by foreign officials has been held except the period of cold relationships surrounding 2012 confrontations.

There have been collaborations at officials of aid agencies. According to the monthly journal of JBIC,[6] JBIC and China EXIM have long had

---

[6] JBIC China Report, No. 1, 2016. This is a Japanese publication.

professional meetings among the officials of the two official banks and in the framework of Asian Bankers' Group. JBIC was a successor organization of Japan EXIM. What is equally important, JBIC sanctioned some money to China EXIM as a credit line. It is an example of JBIC's financial collaboration or co-financing with other official banking institutions around the world. JBIC has had a Memorandum of Understanding (MOU) with the Bank of Brazil to invest in Africa.[7]

In addition, when the author visited a research institute of a municipal office of Tianjin, China, in 2010, he was introduced to a lady who was a teaching staff member of a university in Tianjin. She told the author that her university had received support from JICA office in China for training African trainees. The Chinese university appreciated technical and financial support from the JICA office. No details have been obtained from JICA.

---

[7] One example of this collaboration is investment in Nacara Corridor in the north of Mozambique, a former Portuguese colony. A Brazilian multinational enterprise (MNE) invested in coal mine with Japanese Mitsui & C. (one of the largest in the sector) in the region. Prime Minister Abe announced an aid to the project on his visit to the country in 2014.

Chapter 5

Contest between Japan and China from 2012 to 2020s

This chapter will examine in depth latest developments and future directions of a contest in aid to SSA by the long-term governments of Prime Minister Abe and of General Secretary Xi until early 2020s.

5.1 Rival Administrations of Japan and China

5.1.1 *Abe Administration*

(1) Before Abe's Second Administration since December 2012

Before the establishment of Abe administration in December 2012, there were high-level meetings arranged for the two countries. Abe who was Prime Minister from 2006 to 2007 and Aso, Prime Minister from 2008 to 2009, and current vice Prime Minister of Abe's second administration, were engaged.

(a) High Level Economic Dialogue

On his official visit to Japan in April 2007, Wen, Premier of the State Council (Government) agreed to hold high-level Economic Dialogue with Japan. The ministerial level meeting was also attended by Abe and Aso. The first Dialogue was held in Beijing in December the same year. It was chaired by Vice Premier of the State Council and Foreign Minister of Japan. The communiqué includes the following dialogue on Africa:

"VI. Others
(African Development)
2. The two sides shared the recognition of the importance of African development and decided to continue the dialogue. In this regard, the Chinese side expressed its intent to seriously consider sending a delegation to TICAD IV scheduled to be held in Japan next year."

The second Dialogue was held in Beijing in June 2009. It was attended by Wang, one of top eight members of the Politburo. The third Dialogue was held in August 2010. In the communiqué, there were issues on global and regional cooperation and their challenges. In addition to constructive exchange of views toward the success of the 16th session of the Conference of the Parties (COP16), the two sides agreed to advance bilateral dialogue on assistance for a third country,

There has not been any more Dialogue since 2010. Vice Premier of the State Council showed reluctance to hold the fourth Economic Dialogue. When Abe had a summit meeting with Li, Premier in December 2015, they agreed to hold the meeting in early 2016. The vice minister cited deterioration of political relationships between the two countries for the reason.

(b) Japan–China–ROK Trilateral Summit Meeting
According to the *Blue Book* on Japan's diplomacy published by Japan's Foreign Ministry, there has been a Japan–China–ROK Trilateral Summit Meeting since 2008. Prime Minister Aso of the LDP invited Premier Wen of State Council, China, and President Lee Myung-bak of the ROK to Japan and hosted the first formal Japan–China–ROK Trilateral Summit Meeting. The meeting was held every year until 2012.

The three country leaders' meetings had been held earlier during the period from 1999 to 2007. Those meetings were held in association with ASEAN+3 Summit Meetings. Prime Minister Aso's initiative was to hold independent meetings between the three countries. The meetings were held annually from 2008 to 2012. There were ministerial meetings and professional experts' meetings as well as the leaders' meetings. A policy dialogue on African development was one of the meetings.

The tripartite meeting was suspended because of maritime territorial disputes between Japan and China in 2012. But it was resumed in 2015, for the first time after establishment of Abe's second administration in December 2012. In March 2015, the Japan–China–ROK Foreign Ministers' Meeting was held for the first time in three years.

(c) Territorial Arrangements

On the political side, there was a move from Japan and China to avoid confrontation on territorial issues as shown in the case of an island Shirakaba (Chinese name: Chunxiao). There are oil and gas fields in deep sea around the island. Both parties issued Japan–China Joint Press Statement on Cooperation between Japan and China in the East China Sea in June 2008. However, after the confrontation over Senkaku in 2012, the cooperation for Shirakaba has not developed since then. There has been unilateral action by China to develop the island.

(2) Abe Administration

(a) Policy Stance

Abe won a general election with an overwhelming majority on December 25, 2012. It was a humiliating defeat for the DP which was in power only from 2009 to 2012. Abe had won another election in 2016. DP lost again and was marginalized.

Abe has been popular mainly because of his economic policies. Three groups of policies, which are called Abenomics, have enhanced Japanese economy. The policies taken were monetary easing, fiscal stimulus and structural reforms. The economy recovered from low growth rates after "Lost Decade" in the 1990s and negative impact of Global Financial Crisis since 2008.

Since his election in December 2012, Abe proposed very active foreign policy and took many overseas trips. Visiting about 70 countries in three years, he has developed good personal relationships with many leaders from Vladimir Putin to Donald Trump and those of emerging and developing countries, but except those of China and South Korea.

Abe had visited China one month after the establishment of his first cabinet in 2006. But his relationship in the second cabinet since December 2012 was not good. There were two reasons. First, nationalization of the disputed islands triggered extensive rioting in many cities in China in September 2012. It was one of the worst demonstrations against Japanese goods and properties in China.

Second, China was suspicious about historical views of Abe and his administration about Japan's war against China in World War II.[1] Abe went to Yasukuni Shrine on December 26, 2013, just one year after his election as Prime Minister. This visit exacerbated the relations with China and South Korea.

Abe recently proposed an amendment of the Constitution by 2020 which would stipulate inclusion of defense forces. There may be strong reaction to this move from China and South Korea.

(b) Strategy for Exports of Infrastructure
On the economic front, the Abe administration announced a strategy for exports of infrastructure techniques and management skills together with hardware in May 2013. Prime Minister Abe reiterated "quality infrastructure" at international meetings. This is an antithesis to voluminous investment in infrastructure by China. The objective is 3 trillion yen or 300 billion U.S. dollars by 2020.

This initiative reflects a desire of Japan's top enterprises. Keidanren, a federation of top enterprises, made a statement as follows:

> *"The high quality and disaster resilient features of Japan's infrastructure systems are highly recognized by the international community. To contribute further to the international community by disseminating these systems, the Japanese Government needs to enhance the leadership function of its Ministerial Meeting on Strategy relating Infrastructure Export and Economic Cooperation and to offer a proper combination of technologies and financing by fully reflecting private-sector needs."*[2]

The organizations in question are the JBIC, the overseas investment and financing by the JICA and the insurance service by the NEXI, and

---

[1] Congressional Research Service, *Japan-U.S. Relations: Issues for Congress*, January 13, 2015. It was also reported that Obama administration regarded him as a revisionist.
[2] Keidanren, *Policy Proposals: International Cooperation, Towards Strategic Promotion of the Infrastructure Export*. http://www.keidanren.or.jp/en/policy/2015/105.html

Japan Overseas Infrastructure Investment Corporation for Transport & Urban Development (JOIN). When Abe presided the G7 summit meeting in Japan in 2016, the communiqué included this quality investment. It was a diplomatic victory for Abe administration.

In the latest developments, JBIC announced a loan agreement with the Iraqi government.[3] It is the first in 31 years. The bank together with two large Japanese banks will give a loan of 530 million U.S. dollars to buy electrical facilities. JBIC had opened a special account for risky projects to counter loans by AIIB led by China.

The background is that Japanese companies compete with Chinese and Korean enterprises. In fact, the Japanese enterprises cannot compete with them because of their low-cost proposals for infrastructure development. According to the Nikkei news, the Japan's Government thinks emerging countries may pay attention to quality offered by Japanese enterprises. The latest G20 statement in 2017 included a necessity of quality infrastructure advocated by Japan.

5.1.2 *Xi Administration*

As already explained in Sections 3.1.2 and 4.1.1, Xi became the top leader of China in November 2012. He was selected General Secretary of the Communist Party at the Committee Meeting, then Head of State in March the following year. It should be noted that his October election included chairman of the Military Committee. He could gain command over the military forces in the country immediately.

In China, the chairman can preside for five years. There will be another committee meeting scheduled in November 2017. His predecessors Hu had two terms from 2002 to 2007 and from 2007 to 2012. At the time of writing, many assume that Xi will be reelected in November 2017.

One noteworthy point about Xi's leadership is that Xi was called "core leader" in 2016. This happened one year before the start of his second

---

[3] Nihonkeizai Shimbun (daily newspaper), *Infra yushutu he kousei* (Toward more infrastructure exports), Nihonkeizai Shimbun, May 31, 2017. In Table 2-7 in Chapter 2 of this book, it is interesting that Iraq was a top recipient of Japan's ODA. The assistance was in the form of grant. The country was one of major countries for the Fragile States Initiative led by the U.S. and the U.K.

tenure. This term dates back a few decades only and has been given to four leaders only: Mao Zedong, Deng Xiaoping, Jiang Zemin and now Xi. This may mean strong leadership of Xi or that power structures were centralized around him. It is true that he could strengthen his leadership because of his strong anti-corruption campaigns since his election in 2012.

It is reported, however, that it was on the contrary to the preceding regime under Hu where a group consultation system was introduced by him. There is a report that the term "core" is needed to establish his leadership which is not that strong.[4]

5.1.3 *Close Competition in Aid to Africa*

(1) Competition in General

Since the establishment of Abe administration in September 2012, no state visit has been made between the two leaders. They have held the following summit meetings on occasions of international conferences:

(1) In Beijing, at APEC forum in November 2014;
(2) In Indonesia on the occasion of Bandung anniversary in April 2015;
(3) In Hangzhou, China, at G20 summit in September 2016;
(4) In Peru, at APEC forum in Lima, November 2016.

As explained, one reason for no official visit is that there was a water territorial issue which became serious in 2012. Xi was elected in November 2012 soon after serious anti-Japan rioting in China in September 2012. Another is that it is his first tenure of five years for Xi from 2012. He may have tried to be tough against Japan to consolidate his power base within the party and the government.

Abe's stance for historical issues has been questioned by the Chinese side. His visit to Yasukuni Shrine in December 2013 made the relationships deteriorate. In 2015, Abe was invited to make an official visit to China and to attend a ceremony commemorating the 70th anniversary of China's

---

[4] Jiang and Xi came from Shanghai groups. Xi's deputy, Li is prime minister. He had belonged to Youth League of the Communist Party from which Hu, Xi's predecessor, originated.

victory over Japanese Army in September 2015. Eventually, Abe announced a postponement of his state visit to avoid his attendance of the ceremony.

His pledges of aid to developing countries were too big compared to its annual budgets of external assistance or aid as explained in Chapter 3. According to the DAC reports, the latest figure was 3 billion U.S. dollars in 2015. There have been substantial loans by China EXIM and other banks in addition to "ODA-like." The size of the loans could be three to five times those of "ODA-like."

Based on this reality, it seems that China may not think Japan as a rival in aid to developing countries. The country may think it should match the top donor, which is the U.S. As explained, China has held annual Economic Dialogue since 2005 and Strategic and Economic Dialogue afterwards. At the latest annual Dialogue in 2015, China proposed that the two countries should regard themselves as equal giant powers in the world. The U.S. did not accept it, though. The latest summit meeting between Xi and Trump followed suit. In this sense, it is worth making reference to the relationships between China and U.S.

(2) Competition in the African Context

(a) Exchanges of Pledges at TICAD and FOCAC

There was a competition in aid to Africa at TICAD and FOCAC levels by Japan and China. As explained in Introduction of this book, the two countries competed between themselves to appeal to Africa and international aid community. While Xi, General Secretary of the Communist Party pledged 60 billion U.S. dollars in December 2015, Abe, Prime Minister of Japan, announced 30 billion U.S. dollars which was an addition to 32 billion U.S. dollars at the previous meeting held three years back — altogether 62 billion U.S. dollars.

As regards to TICAD VI held in August 2016, Abe pledged an amount of approximately 30 billion U.S. dollars under public-private partnership for a period of three years from 2016 to 2018. Priorities were given to development of quality infrastructure, building of resilient health systems, and forging of the foundations for peace and stability in the continent.

The important slogan was empowerment and quality. Making "Quality Africa," it was announced that Japan would utilize its high levels of science, technologies and innovation.[5] At that time, Foreign Minister Kishida stressed aid in quality against quantity championed by China. Abe had hosted the G7 Ise-Shima Summit in which the joint statement included quality infrastructure.

On the side of China's FOCAC, the composition of the pledge in 2015 was given in the following statement of the State Council of China:

"To ensure smooth implementation of the initiatives, Xi announced, China will offer 60 billion U.S. dollars of funding support, including 5 billion dollars of free aid and interest-free loans, 35 billion dollars of preferential loans and export credit on more favorable terms, 5 billion dollars of additional capital for the China-Africa Development Fund and the Special Loan for the Development of African SMEs each, and a China-Africa production capacity cooperation fund with the initial capital of 10 billion dollars."[6]

The pledge of the previous conference in 2012 was 20 billion U.S. dollars. The pledge in 2015 was far larger than the annual aid budget or external assistance for all developing countries recorded in the *Finance Book of the Government of China*. As discussed in Chapter 3, the latest trends were about 3 billion dollars only. The amount "35 billion U.S. dollars of preferential loans and export credit on more favorable terms" may be financial aid by China EXIM. When one think about China's aid, it is important to refer to activities of China EXIM bank. "OOF-like" may be loans by China EXIM. Its low interest loans for "ODA-like" were unknown as well.

(b) Latest Developments
The pledge made by Xi at the last FOCAC conference in December 2015 has already been realized by 2017 as follows:

"Already China has expended over 50 percent of the 60 billion dollars given to fund projects in the 10 cooperation plans outlined by President Xi

---

[5] Japan's measures for Africa at TICAD VI "Quality and Empowerment." http://www.mofa.go.jp/files/000183835.pdf
[6] Huaxia, "Xi announces 10 major China-Africa cooperation plans for coming 3 years." English. news.cn, December 4, 2015. http://news.xinhuanet.com/english/2015-12/04/c_134886420.htm

at the Johannesburg Summit of the Forum on China-Africa Cooperation (FOCAC) held in South Africa in December 2015. The good news is that the process of China and Africa deepening engagement on the decisive infrastructure challenge of the continent will receive a massive boost and will be further mainstreamed in the framework of the Belt and Road Initiative."[7]

This "One Belt, One Road" (OBOR) project was first announced by Xi in November 2014. There are two main routes: a silk road on land from China to Europe and a maritime silk road connecting China to Europe. Eastern parts of Africa are part of the latter.

The author includes information on "One Belt, One Road" project given that his visit to Shanghai in May 2017 coincided with its summit meeting held in Beijing. The project has already been endorsed by the United Nations, the EU and OAU. The Kenyan President and the Ethiopian Prime Minister attended the summit meeting in Beijing. Djibouti has already opened a Silk Road Fund and is very active in promoting the project. Kenya will celebrate a railway between Nairobi and Mombasa port built by China. OBOR will further be discussed for Djibouti and Kenya as case studies in Chapter 6.

Xi visited Tanzania and the Republic of Congo when he visited RSA for a summit meeting of BRICS in 2014. It was his first visit to Africa after the establishment of his regime in March 2013. Referring to Tazara (Tanzania–Zambia) Railway built with China's aid (see Section 3.2.1), he stressed cordial relationships with Tanzania. Its Bagamoyo port is part of China's "String of Pearls" strategy which surrounds the Indian Ocean. The building of a port costs 10 billion U.S. dollars. The "String of Pearls" strategy was proposed in the early 2000s by U.S. researchers.[8] It reflects Chinese investment in ports along the Indian Ocean, which looks like the "string of pearls."

---

[7] Onunaiju, C., "Belt & Road Special: Inclusive Approach: Global Integration Strategy Can Address Africa's Infrastructure and Employment Woes," *Beijing Review*, May 11, 2017, Vol. 60, No. 19.

[8] The Center for Strategic and International Studies (CSIS) is a nonprofit organization located in Washington, DC. There is the following information in their website: "Revisiting China's 'String of Pearls' Strategy Places 'with Chinese Characteristics' and Their Security Implications," *Issues & Insights*, June 24, 2014, Vol. 14, No. 7. https://www.csis.org/analysis/issues-insights-vol-14-no-7-revisiting-chinas-string-pearls-strategy

Tanzania has been a model case of aid reforms led by Western donors. It has been a major recipient of Japan's ODA. Japan regarded the country as a leading country in African continent. Japan constructed one of the largest rice fields in the outskirts of Mount Kilimanjaro. This big project was comparable to the Matadi Bridge in Congo (see Section 3.2.1). As a "Western donor," moreover, Japan has provided general budget support to the country since 2004.

5.2 Future Policy Directions

5.2.1 *Possibilities of Collaboration between the Two Countries*

(1) Move to Collaboration at Policy Levels

In the first Abe administration, an agreement was reached on strategic cooperation which was proposed by Abe on his official visit to China in October 2006. The high level economic meetings were held three times from 2007 and 2010. The agenda were trade, investment, and joint assistance to third countries.

In addition, Japan held Africa policy consultations with China and South Korea every year during the period 2008–2010.[9] According to MOFA, there was a tripartite meeting between the three countries, Japanese officials explained about the importance of environmental conservation and joint assistance to third countries.

In recent years, however, no state visits were held because of deteriorations of the relationships between the two countries over historical issues and territorial disputes. After the Abe administration established in late December 2012, the summit meetings were held on occasions of international conferences.

Toward the future, Abe will try to stand for the third term in office in 2018. The third term will last in the fall of 2021. Xi's second tenure will end in late 2022. The main purpose of Abe's long reign is to rewrite the Constitution. 2017 saw the 70th anniversary of the Constitution which had been prepared under the occupation of the U.S. after the end of World

---

[9] Sakamoto, K. (author), "Outlook for Japan-China relations," *Nikkei Shimbun*, November 28, 2014.

War II. This has been one of his most important political aspirations. It is this move that may hamper China's relationships with Abe administration in the fear that Japan may have a constitution which allows the country to have its own army. Japan could have only Self Defense Force after the end of World War II. But it is true that the size of the budget of this force is very large.

At professional levels, however, as explained in Chapter 4, JBIC has provided loans to China EXIM. There have been exchanges of information between officials of those development banks of the two countries.

(2) Needs from Private Enterprises

Japan is one of the largest investors in China. The enterprises of both countries have had a long history of joint activities. There are also needs for joint activities at private levels for third countries. It is frequently reported that Japanese enterprises collaborated with Chinese enterprises to invest in developing countries. In January 2016, Mitsui & Co., a leading trading company, commissioned construction of a power station to a Chinese company. This is part of a project for a fire power plant in Oman.[10] In June 2016, Mitsubishi–Tokyo–UFJ Bank provided a loan of 80 billion yen to a China's state-owned company in the context of a hydropower station in Brazil.[11] There are cases of applications to tenders of international organizations like the World Bank. It is a realistic option to cooperate with Chinese companies which are cost competitive. There are needs from Japanese enterprises for cooperation with the Chinese side.

It is important to look at environments surrounding the movement of Japanese involvement in infrastructure development. There was a strong rivalry in finance to infrastructure development in Asia. Creation of AIIB led to confrontation with Japan and the U.S. It now has more than 100 members larger than ADB led by Japan. ADB's largest contribution comes from Japan followed by the U.S. There are strong needs from

---

[10] When Abe visited Oman in 2014, there was a signing of an MOU on the cooperation on their field of technological and research cooperation for oil and gas development in Oman in January 2014.

[11] Kokusai Kaihatsu Journal (International Development Journal), March 2017, p. 24.

Japanese enterprises which would like to establish cooperation with Chinese counterparts.

Regarding their needs for Africa, the latest move is China's big project: One Belt, One Road. One belt is a silk road between China and Europe. African countries are involved in its Maritime Silk Road. Xi announced this plan at an Asia-Pacific Economic Cooperation (APEC) meeting in 2014. It has been endorsed by the United Nations, too.

When the author visited Shanghai in December 2016, he was told by university scholars that most of the subjects heatedly discussed were those about this project. On the author's visit to Shanghai on May 14, 2017, there were summit meetings about the project in Beijing on May 14–15. Most of G7 countries did not send their top officials. But Abe sent Toshihiro Nikai, the most influential figure of the Party, and the second-in-command of the LDP. Nikai said that Japan will support the project and cooperate with China.

Leaders of more than 100 countries and organizations attended the summit. Twenty-eight heads of state and government leaders attended the summit meeting in May, including Putin of Russia and prime ministers from Italy and Spain. Two heads of states came from Africa: Kenyan President Uhuru Kenyatta and Ethiopian Prime Minister Hailemariam Dessalegn.[12] There are strong needs for infrastructure investment in Eastern Africa. The project will be discussed in Chapter 6 on case studies of Djibouti and Kenya.

There were also needs from Chinese enterprises to cooperate with their Japanese counterparts. Though catching up with Japanese companies, they can still appreciate high technology and skills in the field of energy conservation, environmental conservation and management of infrastructure. The author was introduced to a senior official of the State Council (Government of China) in Beijing in 2010. It was an introduction by a senior researcher of a research institute located in Tianjin. The author had had meetings with researchers of this institute from 2008. The senior official shared that he had read what the author had written in the past. Then, he proposed that Japan and China should cooperate by using Japan's finance and technology and China's labor.

---

[12] Xinhua Net, "Xi to attend opening ceremony of Belt and Road forum in May," April 18, 2017. http://news.xinhuanet.com/english/2017-04/18/c_136217663.htm

It can be conceived that Japan's experiences as a global donor and as a top donor for African development can be learnt by Chinese counterparts. Japan's assimilation of its aid practices to Western reforms including evaluations of projects and programs is recommended as a good reference to China.

Japan introduced a full range of evaluation systems for all governmental programs and projects in 2001. The systems and techniques were introduced from those developed among DAC reformers. DAC's five principles and its analytical methods were well introduced to all the activities of JICA and governmental offices. Even if activities of Chinese government are not exposed to eyes of the general public, it is important to plan, implement and evaluate programs and projects for success in its activities.

5.2.2 Contest Further?

To look at environments surrounding the two countries, as stated in Chapters 1 and 2, Western new aid practices are rooted deeply in African countries. But it may have lost their significance. This is because private funds are more important than official aid and that non-DAC donors led by China provide more financial assistance than traditional DAC donors.

It is also important to note that China has tried to assimilate international standards of aid including Western aid reforms. As a giant economy in the world, China is trying to be responsible for global and regional affairs in the world. The country cooperated to reach an agreement on COP in Paris in 2015. The country had not shown any sacrifice in COP in the international conference in Copenhagen in 2013. China has had annual top-level meetings with the U.S. and the U.K. Through the consultations, China has realized importance of standards and codes in relation to aid to developing countries including Africa.

In addition, establishment of AIIB and BRICS bank is important. AIIB now comprises more than 100 countries including major developed countries. Only the U.S. and Japan have not joined as major industrial countries. The two countries have expressed concerns over transparency and standards of loan activities of AIIB like environmental conservation and sustainability. China has requested the two countries to join the bank. In this regard, it is now understood that AIIB has worked well with reference to standards and codes of aid at international levels.

In December 2016, the author made a presentation on economic cooperation and aid by Japan and China at a research institute in Shanghai. In response, a Chinese researcher commented that AIIB top officials were very serious about the international-level standard.[13]

As regards to relationships with Trump administration of the U.S., becoming a member of AIIB is an issue. Japan cooperated with the U.S. to give pressure on China's AIIB. There may be a possibility that the two countries may join the AIIB even if there is the ADB led by Japan. In fact, there are pressures from private enterprises so that Japan may join AIIB before the U.S. The Japanese companies are faced with fierce competition from their Chinese and Korean counterparts. The private enterprises may be in favor of application to AIIB and other international organizations including the World Bank, jointly made with Chinese as well as Korean enterprises. This collaboration will be applied to projects in Africa.

Paying attention to domestic factors of the two countries, with a long regime of Abe projected, there may be improvements in economic relations with China at top levels in the future. With changes in tenures of the presidency of the ruling LDP, Abe is likely to remain in power until 2021. There will be an election for General Secretary of LDP in fall 2018. This long rule seems to affect Chinese attitudes toward him. Hostile at first, they may now think that China should seek cooperation with Japan under Abe's rule in the medium term.

Xi may have taken a cautious look at the political stance of Abe administration from Xi's election in late 2012. After Abe's visit to Yasukuni Shrine on December 26, 2013, the relationships deteriorated. Xi may have been less coercive after LDP decided to change terms of Chairmanship of the party from two to three terms. This is because his presidency was in the first tenure from 2012 to 2017. He is expected to have another five-year term until 2022. Xi may think that he should cope with Abe in the medium term.

Finally, as an advanced donor in Asia, Japan can share its experiences as a "Western donor" with China as an emerging donor. The framework of country-level policy and aid coordination can be shared by Chinese counterparts.

---

[13] The author also received a strong comment that negative impact of China's aid on the development of Africa was a fake news created by some journalists.

Chapter 6

Case Studies

6.1 Djibouti: Japanese Army versus Chinese Army

There is a contest in aid to Djibouti. Djibouti is a former French colony. Leading to the Red Sea, this tiny country (which population was 0.9 million in 2005) is strategically important. France, the U.S. and Japan have had permanent military presences in the country. The Japanese navy started using its port facility in 2011, their first foreign base since the end of World War II. Its mission was to protect Japanese vessels against piracy activities in the region. These activities have been also conducted by forces from India, Russia and some of European countries.

China has established a small military base in the country. They moved troops to the country in 2016 to construct the first overseas naval base in the Gulf of Tadjoura. China invests massively in the country. The infrastructure projects include the Ethiopia–Djibouti railway, a new multipurpose port, and a free trade zone — scheduled to open in January 2018 — as well as a liquefied natural gas terminal. Looking at Table 6-1 based on an IMF report, one can understand easily how large their investments were.

The railway which cost 4.2 billion U.S. dollars was opened in January 2017. It stretches 470-mile line from Djibouti to Addis Ababa, the capital of Ethiopia. The project replaced a French-built railway built about 100 years ago. China's investment in Ethiopia was explained in Chapter 3, which included relocation of Chinese industries in Ethiopia.

Table 6-1 China's Investment in Djibouti (2016)

	Total Cost (Mn U.S.$)	Financing	Financing Source
Main Investment Projects Contracted (Transportation)			
Addis Ababa–Djibouti Railway	490	Publicly guaranteed debt	China EXIM
Port de Goubet	64	Publicly guaranteed debt	China EXIM
Multipurpose Port Doraieh	580	Public Debt	China EXIM
Planned Investment Projects			
Addis Ababa–Djibouti railway electrification	24	Publicly guaranteed debt	China EXIM
Djibouti new international airport	450	Publicly guaranteed debt	China EXIM
Obock international airport	200	FDI	China EXIM
Road Djibouti–Galileh	580	Public Debt	China EXIM
Liquefied natural gas (LNG) pipeline	3,000	FDI	China EXIM
Darmerjog port crude oil terminal	200	Publicly guaranteed debt	China

Source: IMF, *Article IV Consultation Report*, February 2017.

IMF has expressed concern over the huge investment in Djibouti by China and the country's debt sustainability. The *Staff Report for the 2016 Article IV Consultation* raises the following key issues in February 7, 2017:

"Context. Djibouti is expanding its infrastructure to leverage its strategic location and foster growth, reduce poverty, and create jobs. The remarkable investments in ports and railways — started in 2015 and mostly debt-financed by financial institutions from China — presents opportunities as well as risks. With public debt rising from 50 to 85 percent of GDP in just two years, the authorities need to advance rapidly with critical reforms. Such reforms would aim at translating the investment boom into strong, inclusive, and job-creating growth to reduce poverty and return to a sustainable debt trajectory given the current high risk of debt distress."

Table 6-2 Debt Sustainability of Djibouti

	World Bank: International Debt Statistics, December 2016				IMF: Staff Report for 2016 Article IV Consultation, February 2017			
	2012	2013	2014	2015	2015	2016 (proj..)	2017 (proj..)	2018 (proj..)
External Debt (Stock)	642	673	820	1,169	1,197	1,610	1,814	2,008
Public Debt					495	508		
Multilateral					323	322		
Official Bilateral					172	186		
Paris Club					47	47		
Non-Paris Club					125	139		
Publicly-Guaranteed Debt					696	1,096		
Stock of External Arrears					6			
Public & Publicly-Guaranteed Debt (in Percent of GDP)					69.3	84.8	86.9	87.3

Sources: World Bank, *International Debt Statistics 2017.*
IMF, *Staff Report for the 2016 Article IV Consultation,* February 2017.

The name of China is clearly stated in the above statement. Table 6-2 shows remarkable increase in debt.

In fact, it was in February 2014 that the country and China reached a military agreement so that Chinese navy could use the port facilities. The debt problem had already been cited in the IMF *Staff Report for the 2014 Article IV Consultation*. It raises the following key issues in January 15, 2015 as follows:

> "CONTEXT
> 1. Djibouti is undergoing a debt-financed investment boom. Major investments currently in progress include an extension of facilities at the state-owned ports as well as the building of new ports, financed in part by private investors; and the construction of a railway linking Djibouti and neighboring landlocked Ethiopia, and a pipeline to transport potable water from Ethiopia (Annex II). The government is financing both the railway and water pipeline projects mainly through nonconcessionary foreign debt, aggravating medium-term fiscal and external debt vulnerabilities."

Impact of nonconcessional loans on budgetary and BOP balances were worrying. In this report, IMF also stated that Djibouti faces widespread poverty with high levels of unemployment despite high economic growth motivated by huge investments in port and related facilities. Per capita gross national income (GNI) was 1,030 U.S. dollars in 2005.

Djibouti is also part of the OBOR project by China. This grand project was first announced by Xi in November 2014. Its first summit meeting was held in Beijing in May 14–15, 2017 while the author was in Shanghai. One of the two main routes to Europe is a maritime silk road which passes Eastern parts of Africa. Djibouti has already opened a Silk Road Fund. OBOR will further be discussed in the next section on Kenya.

6.2 Kenya: Top Recipient of Japan's ODA versus Maritime Silk Road from China

Kenya has been an important country for Western countries in the period of the Cold War. Many African countries adopted a pro-Eastern diplomacy with socialistic government-led economic strategies, represented by Tanzania and Ghana. On the other hand, Kenya took a pro-Western policy with relatively market-oriented economic approaches. Its strategic position was very important in the time of West–East confrontations.

Kenya has been important for Japan's ODA, too. The country was the biggest recipient of Japan's loans by 2014. Its cumulative total was 330.629 billion U.S. dollars against 1,879.682 billion U.S. dollars for all SSA countries. That is why the first TICAD conference in Africa was held in Nairobi in August 2016. The second largest was Ghana. Japan has had a long history of various types of aid for Kenya. It has become a hub for Japan's third country training.

One of the most successful technical assistance projects of Japan's ODA was Strengthening Mathematics and Science Education Project (SMASE) in Kenya. The overall goal of the project is to upgrade:

— Capability of primary and secondary school pupils in mathematics and science; and
— Teaching skills of school teachers in mathematics and science.

The project was so successful that the outcome spread all over the country. In addition, SMASE projects were implemented in many other African countries like Nigeria and Malawi (explained later). It should be added that Kenya whose GNI per capita was 1,340 U.S. dollars in 2015 started attracting various types of private investment from Japan. When the author visited Kenya in 1983, there were branch offices of Tokyo Bank (only special bank for foreign exchange) and of Japan Airline. But they had left the country because of debt crises in the 1980s and 1990s.

Going back to the OBOR Project, when the author was in Shanghai in May 2017, its first summit meeting was held in Beijing on May 14–15. The author had been told that there were many meetings and seminars about the project during his visit to Shanghai in December 2016. Twenty-eight heads of state attended the summit in May which included Russian President Putin and Recep Tayyip Erdoğan, President of Turkey. Of major European countries, only prime ministers of Italy and Spain were present. Kenyan President Uhuru Muigai Kenyatta was the only top-level African VIP. It is noteworthy that Ethiopian Prime Minister Hailemariam Desalegn Boshe also attended the summit.

As stated in Chapter 5, the project was announced at an APEC meeting in November 2014. More than 100 countries have supported and/or concluded agreements on cooperation. It has been endorsed by the Security Council of the United Nations, its General Assembly, Association of Southeast Asian Nations (ASEAN), Arab League, the EU, OAU, and so on. Abe administration declared that Japan would support the project.

According to the statement made by the Government of China in March 2015, there are the following three routes:

— Beijing–Russia–Germany–Northern Europe;
— Xi'an–Ürümqi–Afghanistan–Kazakhstan–Hungary–Paris; and
— Guangzhou–Hanoi–Kuala Lumpur–Sri Lanka–Nairobi–Athens–Geneva.

The last maritime silk road in the 21st century stretches to Mombasa, Nairobi, Djibouti and Ethiopia. In this region, China has tried to build regional rail networks. As explained earlier, China heralded in January 2017 a 470-mile railway from Djibouti to Addis Ababa. The project cost 4.2 billion U.S. dollars. This linked a sea port of Djibouti to the landlocked capital of Ethiopia. In Kenya, China is building a new railway that will run 300 miles between Nairobi, also landlocked, and the Indian Ocean port of Mombasa. It costs another 4 billion U.S. dollars. The Government of Kenya will finance 10 percent of the rail project, with the remainder financed by China EXIM Bank. This railway may stretch to inland countries of Uganda and Rwanda in the future.[1] The Kenyan railway will be open to traffic on May 31, 2017.

6.3 Malawi: Japan's Grassroots Support versus Nation Building by China

It is often reported that China gives aid to Africa in return of natural resources. It is worth analyzing a case of a resource-poor country like Malawi. This small landlocked country had a population of 17 million in 2015. It is one of the lowest income countries in the world with per capita GNI of 340 U.S. dollars in 2015. The economy which depends on smallholder agriculture was exposed to high population growth of more than 3 percent per annum and frequent climatic disturbances. The author worked for the Economic Planning Office for the Government of Malawi as a macro-economist dispatched by the United Nations during the period of 1983–1987. The export structure is still the same as that time: tobacco, sugar and tea only.

Malawi has been a priority country for Japan's ODA. JOCVs have been sent since 1971. About 2,000 young men and women came for assistance from many regions of Japan. There were 104 volunteers in 2015. JOCVs' model was that of American Peace Corps with about 120 American volunteers.

As explained earlier about Kenya, Malawi also deploys SMASE projects around the country. It is also noted that the country started in 2003 "One Village, One Product" (OVOP) project originating from Oita in Kyushu Island in Japan. This is one of the most successful private-led

---

[1] "China's investment in Kenya in recent years is massive. Finance and expertise from Beijing are crucial to Kenyatta's infrastructure spree," *Financial Times*, April 3, 2017. https://www.ft.com/content/d0fd50ee-1549-11e7-80f4-13e067d5072c

project which was implemented around the world. Several places in China also implement this project supported by the Ministry of Industry of the Government of Japan.

The OVOP project or program is a community centered and demand-driven regional economic development approach initiated by Oita prefecture in Japan in the 1970s. Malawi and Cameroon are most active in the project, sending a number of delegations and trainees to Oita.

The diplomatic ties with Mainland China was established only in 2007. After independence, Malawi took ultra-rightist diplomatic policies, taking sides with Taiwan as well as Israel and South Africa. Malawi was the last to move to a democratic regime, holding a multiparty election in 1994 for the first time. The subsequent leaders had objected to recognition of the Beijing Government in China, sticking to warm ties with Taiwan for more than 40 years. While the author worked in Malawi from 1983 to 1987, there were Taiwanese missions active in the field of agriculture (rice and vegetables).

China's investment since then was enormous. To look at recent contests between Japan and China for Malawi, there were the following reports based on monthly reports in Japanese published by the Embassy of Japan in Lilongwe:

November 4, 2015
The Japanese Embassy concluded a grant aid of 36 million dollars.
((Daily Newspaper) Nation November 5)

November 24, 2015
(China's) Deputy Ambassador revealed that China had given low interest loans for International Conference Hall and five-star hotel worth 110 million dollars, National Stadium 60 million, Polytechnic University 80 million. (Nation Nov. 26 Daily Times)http://www.nyasatimes.com/2016/01/31/

January 31, 2016
China's Foreign Minister visited Malawi and announced 9 million dollars for emergency food aid, 16 grant for modernization of agriculture, 8 million as a soft loan, altogether 35 million.

March 26, 2017

China's grant assistance for construction of five community vocational training schools with 1.5 million dollars, agricultural technology center with 0.2 million, so on. (Daily Times, March 27)

The amounts of China's aid were very large compared to Japan's. In the past, however, Japan tried to show its contribution to Malawi, focusing on construction of an international airport in Lilongwe in late 1970s. The construction cost of about 50 million U.S. dollars was done with 50 percent of loans from Japan and another half from AfDB. Many donors objected to this big project for this low-income country. The loans by Japan were relieved because of its enormous debt burden which was unattainable.

Aid to Malawi by Japan nowadays is the same as that of other Western donors. Its ODA levels ranged from 30 million U.S. dollars to 55 U.S. dollars between 2011 and 2013 (net expenditure). All are given in grants.

Table 6-3 shows composition of external debt stock. Japan's debt may be very low or zero just the same way as other DAC countries. China

Table 6-3 Malawi: Public and Publicly-Guaranteed External Debt

	2013 % Share	2014 % Share	2015 Actual Million U.S.$	2015 % Share
Multilateral	69.85	75.22	1,324.10	75.33
IMF	13.69	9.75	162.81	9.13
IDA	28.78	27.79	589.90	33.09
ADF	13.19	12.52	228.77	12.83
Others	14.19	25.16	342.62	20.28
Bilateral	28.58	23.97	439.48	24.65
France	0.75	0.18	0.00	0.00
Belgium	0.15	0.11	1.72	0.10
Mainland China	17.44	13.52	242.74	13.61
India	7.34	7.86	151.74	8.51
Others	2.90	2.30	43.28	2.43
Total	100.00	100.00	1,782.97	100.00

Source: IMF, *Malawi: Debt Sustainability Analysis*, June 3, 2016.

together with India has very high levels of debt for Malawi. For example, China EXIM provided 80 million U.S. dollars for construction of a university for science and technology in a rural area. But a highway linking the northern town of Karonga to a border town with Zambia was constructed with a grant of 70 million dollars. The huge amounts of investment by China contribute to nation building of Malawi. Though small, Japan's ODA takes into account actual capacity of Malawi to mobilize limited resources and may produce tangible results at grassroots levels. In aid reforms of DAC countries, a shift from university education to primary or secondary education has been proposed for low-income countries like Malawi. That is why Japan has tried to implement SMASE projects in many African countries.

Chapter 7

Concluding Remarks

Japan's economic development was called a miracle of the Orient. In foreign aid, it became the largest donor in the world in 1989 and — with the exception of 1990 — remained so until 1999. Constrained partly by the Japanese Constitution drafted under the U.S. occupation after the end of World War II, the Japanese government could only exert its influence over world issues on the basis of its economic strength.

As a late-comer in the field of providing aid to developing countries, Japan's ODA placed emphasis on financial aid by mode, investment in infrastructure by sector, and Asian countries by geography. To gain more influence and acquire a permanent seat on the United Nations Security Council, Japan was engaged more actively in global issues through its foreign aid. This action was partly assisted by the U.S., which wanted to utilize Japan's financial resources.

Following this policy, Japan became an important donor to SSA. It established the TICAD in 1993, when other Western donors were actually decreasing their aid to Africa. TICAD was held every five years until 2013, when it was held in 2016 after three years. It was frequently reported that the Japanese government held TICAD to gain support of African countries for securing a permanent seat on the United Nations Security Council.

China's economic growth was more spectacular than Japan's. Growing at annual rates of about 10 percent for 20 years since the early 1990s, China toppled Japan to become the second-largest economy in 2010. Its real GDP also surpassed that of the U.S. in 2015. Absorbing about half of the global investment (non-financial) flows from abroad in 2014, the giant country became a net exporter of capital in 2015. It increased its official aid substantially, corresponding to its continuous export increase since the 1980s and the high growth of its FDI abroad in the mid-2000s. China also started the FOCAC, a ministerial forum, in 2000, with meetings being held every three years.

Abe became the Prime Minister of Japan in December 2012, and Xi was elected the General Secretary of the Chinese Communist Party in November of the same year. Their elections were conducted just after serious confrontations arose between the two countries over disputed islands in September 2012. There were strong demonstrations against Japanese premises, related businesses, and Japanese nationals in 50 cities around China.

The aforementioned developments — together with the relationship between the two countries, which had not been cordial since the early 2000s because of historical as well as maritime territory issues — have made the rivalry between the two newly established administrations intense. With high growth rates in African countries in the 21st century, private capital has replaced official aid and emerging donors are being led by China against traditional Western donors. Japan, meanwhile, attuned its aid policies to Western aid reforms after the end of the Cold War.

China has established a tremendous presence in Africa in recent years. Japan has tried to counter China's influence by highlighting the quality of its investments to the international community and developing countries, which may be an antithesis to China's voluminous aid to Africa. Japan's attitude of superiority may have arisen because Japan has become one of the most advanced countries in the world and a member of the G7 and the DAC of the OECD.

The latest FOCAC summit meeting was held in December 2015, wherein President Xi pledged 60 billion U.S. dollars in foreign aid to Africa for three years. Eight months later, Japan responded by hosting TICAD (three years after the last one, instead of five years) in Nairobi, Kenya. Prime Minister Abe pledged 30 billion U.S. dollars in foreign aid to Africa, in addition to 32 billion U.S. dollars announced in Yokohama in 2013. China's pledge was disproportionately large compared with its annual budget of bilateral "ODA-like" flows of around 3 billion U.S. dollars. The Export–Import Bank of China and other development banks provided substantial loans, sometimes more than three times the amount of "ODA-like" flows.

Prime Minister Abe initiated a strategy of infrastructure export in 2013. There has been an ongoing competition in providing aid to SSA between the Abe and Xi administrations, and this rivalry may continue, with both leaders possibly staying in power until the early 2020s. Given a recent ruling by the LDP to extend the maximum tenure of its president from the current six years to nine, Prime Minister Abe could run for a third term that extends through 2021. Consequently, he intends to rewrite the Japanese Constitution. China has taken the lead in countering Abe's move and intends to make itself more influential, especially in the military field, among other Asian countries. In response, Japan's new Development Charter may stress the continuation of more aid to politically fragile states. In this regard, the relationship between the two countries may not improve as they have critical issues over historical views and maritime territories.

Economically, however, there has been a move to improve the relationship at top levels because the two economies need cooperation to prosper. Japanese enterprises would prefer to cooperate rather than compete with their Chinese and Korean counterparts. Though Chinese institutions and enterprises have assimilated international practices of aid and cooperation with Africa, they are aware that they require high levels of technology, like environmental conservation, for the management of projects in Africa and that China can learn from Japan's experiences to become a leading donor to the West from among developing countries.

References

Beijing Review, "Championing Positive Change," December 22, 2016.

Bautigram, D., *Will Africa Feed China?*, Oxford University Press, 2015.

Brautigam, D., *The Dragon's Gift: The Real Story of China in Africa*, Oxford University Press, 2009.

Center for Strategic and International Studies (CSIS), "Revisiting China's 'String of Pearls' Strategy Places 'with Chinese Characteristics' and Their Security Implications," *Issues & Insights*, June 24, 2014, Vol. 14, No. 7. https://www.csis.org/analysis/issues-insights-vol-14-no-7-revisiting-chinas-string-pearls-strategy

Chen W. *et al.*, "Investment Renaissance," *Finance & Development* (IMF), December 2015, Vol. 52, No. 4.

China Bureau of Statistics, *Statistical Yearbook*, various issues.

Congressional Research Service (U.S.), *Japan-U.S. Relations: Issues for Congress*, January 13, 2015.

DAC/OECD, *Shaping the 21st Century: The Contribution of Development Co-operation*, 1996.

DAC/OECD, *Development Co-operation Report 2016*.

DAC/OECD, Peer Reviews on Japan's ODA, 1995, 2003, 2010, and 2014.

Department of Information Services, *China Yearbook 2011*.

Department of Information Services, *China Yearbook 2012*.

Department of Information Services, *The Republic of China Yearbook 2016*.

Forum on China–Africa Cooperation, FOCAC ABC, 2013/04/09. http://www.focac.org/eng/ltda/ltjj/t933522.htm

IMF, "Theoretical Aspects of the Design of Fund-Supported Adjustment Program," Occasional Paper No. 55, 1987.

IMF, *Financial Programming and Policy: The Case of Turkey*, 2000.
IMF, *World Economic Outlook Database April 2011*.
IMF, *Direction of Trade Statistics 2015*
IMF, *World Economic Outlook April 2016*.
IMF, *Malawi: Debt Sustainability Analysis*, June 3, 2016.
IMF, *Article IV Consultation Report*, February 2017.
IMF, *Staff Report for the 2016 Article IV Consultation*, February 2017.
IMF, *International Financial Statistics*, various issues.
Information Office of the State Council, *China's Foreign Aid 2011*, Beijing.
Information Office of the State Council, *China's Foreign Aid 2014*, Beijing.
Japan Bank for International Cooperation (JBIC), *JBIC China Report*, No. 1, 2016.
Japan Bank for International Cooperation (JBIC), *JBIC China Report*, No. 1, 2016. (in Japanese).
Japan External Trade Organization (JETRO), *Annual Report on World Trade and Investment*, various issues (in Japanese).
Japan International Cooperation Agency (JICA), *Annual Report*, various issues.
Jolly, R. et al., *Adjustment with a Human Face: Protecting the Vulnerable and Promoting Growth v.1*, Clarendon Press, 1987.
Keidanren, *Policy Proposals: International Cooperation, Towards Strategic Promotion of the Infrastructure Export*. http://www.keidanren.or.jp/en/policy/2015/105.html
Kernen, A., & B. Vulliet, "Petits commerçants et entrepreneurs chinois au Mali et au Sénégal," *Afrique contemporaine, Agence française de développement*, 2008-4, numero 228.
Killick, T., *IMF Programmes in Developing Countries: Design and Impact*, Routledge for Overseas Development Institute, 1995.
Mbabia, O., & Wassouni, F. (eds.), *La Présence Chinoise en Afrique Francophone*, Monde Global, 2016.
Ministry of Foreign Affairs (Japan), *The White Paper on Japan's ODA 1994*.
Ministry of Foreign Affairs (Japan), *Cabinet Decision on the Development Cooperation Charter*, February, 2015. http://www.mofa.go.jp/files/000067702.pdf (May 28, 2017).
Ministry of Foreign Affairs (Japan), *Country Handbook 2016*.
Ministry of Foreign Affairs (Japan), *Japan's ODA*, various issues.

Ministry of Foreign Affairs (Japan), *Japan's Assistance Package for Africa at TICAD V*. http://www.mofa.go.jp/files/000006375.pdf

Ministry of Foreign Affairs (Japan), *Japan's Measures for Africa at TICAD VI "Quality and Empowerment"*. http://www.mofa.go.jp/files/000183835.pdf

Mosley, P. et al., *Aid and Power: The World Bank and Policy-Based Lending Volume 1*, Routledge, 1991.

Mosley, P. et al., *Aid and Power: The World Bank and Policy-Based Lending Volume 2 — Case Studies*, Routledge, 1991.

National Bureau of Statistics, *Statistical Yearbook 2016*.

National Bureau of Statistics (China), *Statistical Yearbook*, various issues.

OECD, *Development Co-operation Report, 2015*.

OECD, *Development Co-operation Report*, various issues.

Onunaiju, C., "Belt & Road Special: Inclusive Approach: Global Integration Strategy Can Address Africa's Infrastructure and Employment Woes," *Beijing Review*, May 11, 2017, Vol. 60, No. 19.

Provost, C., "China Publishes First Report on Foreign Aid Policy," *Guardian*, 28 April 2011. https://www.theguardian.com/global-development/2011/apr/28/china-foreign-aid-policy-report (May 21, 2017).

Ramo, J. C., "The Beijing Consensus," The Foreign Policy Centre, 2004. http://fpc.org.uk/fsblob/244.pdf

Routledge, *Europa World Year Book 2013*, October 2012.

Routledge, *Europa World Year Book 2014*.

Sakamoto K., "Balance of Payments Support Aid in Japan," White, H. et al., Evaluating Programme Aid, IDS Bulletin, Volume 27 Issue 4, 1996.

Sakamoto, K. (author), "Outlook for Japan-China relations," *Nikkei Shimbun*, November 28, 2014. (in Japanese).

Toye, J., "Structural Adjustment: Context, Assumptions, Origin and Diversity," Van der Hoeven, R., & Van der Kraaij, F. (eds) *Structual Adjustment and Beyond in Sub-Saharan Africa*, Ministry of Foreign Affairs, the Hague, 1994.

Tsikata, D. et al., "China–Africa Relations: A Case Study of Ghana," A Draft Scoping Study Prepared for the African Economic Research Consortium, Institute of Statistical, Social and Economic Research, University of Ghana, January 2008, pp. 1–28. http://dspace.africaportal.org/jspui/bitstream/123456789/32068/1/Ghana.pdf?1 (May 21, 2017).

UN Economic and Social Council, "Trends in South-South and Triangular Development Cooperation, Background Study for the Development Co-operation Forum," April 2008. www.un.org/ecosoc/docs/pdfs/South-South_cooperation.pdf

UNICEF, *Structural Adjustment with a Human Face*, 1987.

Williamson, J., "From Reform Agenda: A Short History of the Washington Consensus and Suggestions for What to Do Next," *Finance & Development*, September 2003, pp.10–11. https://people.ucsc.edu/~hutch/Econ143/history-wash.pdf (May 13, 2017).

World Bank, *Accelerated Development in Sub-Saharan Africa, An Agenda for Action*, 1981. http://documents.worldbank.org/curated/en/702471468768312009/pdf/multi-page.pdf

World Bank, *Adjustment in Africa, 1994*.

World Bank, *World Bank Guide 2005*.

World Bank, *International Debt Statistics*, December 2015 and 2016.

World Bank, *World Development Indicators 2016*, April 2016.

World Bank, *International Debt Statistics 2017*.

Xinhua Net, http://news.xinhuanet.com/english2010/china/2011-04/21/c_13839683_3.htm (May 17, 2017).

Xinhua Net, http://news.xinhuanet.com/english2010/china/2011-04/21/c_13839683_5.htm (May 17, 2017).

Index

Abe, 72, 90–92, 94–97, 100–108, 110–112, 114
ADB, 49, 111, 114
AFD, 9, 69, 85
Africa, 1, 3, 5, 6, 9–11, 13–15
African development, 1, 3, 13
aid, 1, 2, 3, 5, 7–10, 12–15, 17, 18, 24, 28–40, 42–45, 47, 49, 50, 53, 56–68, 70, 72, 73, 75, 77–88
    aid coordination, 5, 7, 9, 15, 37, 45
    aid reforms, 1, 7, 8, 14
    aid regime, 1, 12, 14, 15
    conditional aid, 1
    condition to aid, 1, 3
    coordination of aid, 15
    dependence on aid, 5
    effectiveness of aid, 7
    financial aid, 18, 34
    foreign aid, 2, 50, 56, 57, 61, 64–66, 68, 72, 73, 77, 79, 81, 84–87
    policies of aid, 1
    project aid, 28
    technical aid, 18, 34
    tied aid, 9, 83

AIIB, 105, 111, 113, 114
APEC, 106, 112, 119
army, 115
ASEAN, 102

Bandung Conference, 49, 74
Beijing Consensus, 47, 73, 80, 81
BRICS, 49
budget support, 7, 8, 25, 28, 37
Bush, 90–92
BWIs, 2, 3, 9–15, 33, 36, 37, 43, 49

China, 47–88
China Development Bank, 69
China EXIM, 14, 28, 31, 45, 61–63, 69, 70, 77, 78, 99, 100, 107, 108, 111, 116, 120, 123
common basket fund, 7, 8, 14, 24, 37, 67
conditionalities, 5–7, 10
COP, 113
COP16, 102
Country Approach, 5

DAC, 7–9, 12, 14, 28, 30, 38, 45, 49, 56–59, 64, 65, 77–79, 82–84, 86, 87, 122, 123

debt
    debt cancellation, 1, 10, 14
    debt crises, 2, 6, 9
    debt relief, 5, 24, 36, 37, 39
    debt rescheduling, 9, 10
democratization, 35, 36
Development Charter, 127
Development Cooperation Charter, 41
Development Cooperation Report, 79, 84
DFID, 9, 98
direct production sectors, 28, 29
Djibouti, 115–119
donor, 5, 7, 9, 10, 14, 15
    bilateral donors, 3
    donor support, 5, 7, 15
    Western donors, 49, 63, 66, 74, 84, 87, 88
DP, 91, 95, 96, 103

East China Sea, 103
economic cooperation, 24, 25, 29, 31, 33, 34, 39, 40, 42–44, 47, 56–58, 67, 77, 81
Economic Dialogue, 101, 102, 107
ESAF, 3, 34
Ethiopia, 115, 117, 119, 120
external assistance, 60, 61, 65
external debt, 3, 12

FDI, 3, 11, 12, 20–22, 24, 27, 30, 38, 53–55, 65, 70, 75, 86
Finance Yearbook, 59–61, 64, 70, 86
FOCAC, 42, 89, 96–98
foreign investment, 2, 3, 11, 14, 15
fragile states, 43
free trade zone, 115
French colony, 115

G7, 7, 10, 13, 24, 37, 38, 40, 45, 92, 105, 108, 112
G20, 105, 106
GDP, 18, 19, 38, 48, 50, 51, 75
general budget support, 28
General Secretary, 67, 71, 72, 93, 96
Ghana, 52, 55, 63
GIIs, 99
grant elements, 30
grants, 14, 15, 58, 61, 64, 84

Hatoyama, 91, 95
HIPC, 12
Hu, 90–95

IBRD, 31, 34
IFS, 53
IMF, 2–7, 11–13, 15, 19–21, 27, 34, 37, 44, 48, 50, 51, 53, 54, 56, 76, 81, 115–118, 122
import liberalization, 13
infrastructure, 2
interest-free loans, 61, 64

Japan EXIM, 31–33
JBIC, 31, 33, 61, 69, 99, 100, 104, 105, 111
JETRO, 55, 56
JICA, 33, 69, 74, 85, 104, 113
JOCV, 58

Kenya, 3, 4, 11, 12, 14, 118–120
Koizumi, 32, 33, 43, 44, 72, 89, 90, 92, 94, 95

LDCs, 80
LDP, 89–92, 94–96, 102, 112, 114
liberal measures, 2, 3

Index

liberalization of markets, 13, 15
lost decade, 6, 18, 21, 30, 38
low-income countries support to government budgets, 7, 8

macro approach, 5, 15
Malawi, 4, 10, 12, 119–123
market-oriented approach, 1, 2, 10, 36
Matadi Bridge, 68, 69
MITI, 32, 44
MNCs, 23, 38
MOFA, 32–35, 43, 44

neoliberalism, 15
NEXI, 33, 104
NGOs, 56, 57
non-DAC countries, 59, 77, 78

OAU, 94, 97, 109, 119
OBOR, 109, 118, 119
ODA, 17, 24, 25, 27–36, 38–45, 47, 56–61, 63, 64, 68–70, 74, 78, 84, 86, 92, 97, 118, 120, 122, 123
  ODA-like, 58–61, 64, 69, 70, 78, 86, 107, 108
ODA Charter, 34, 35, 41, 45
ODI, 54, 86
OECD, 7–9, 12, 26, 30, 38, 49, 56–59, 77, 79, 82–84
OECF, 31–33, 37
OOF, 14, 24, 26–28, 30–33, 39–41, 43, 56–60, 63, 69, 70, 86
  OOF-like, 59, 69, 70, 86, 108

Paris Declaration, 8, 9
Paris Declaration on Aid Effectiveness, 37
peer reviews, 8, 9
PKO, 41, 43

political condition, 10
private flows, 1, 12, 14
program support, 8
project approach, 5
project loan, 8
public sector reform, 6

quality infrastructure, 104, 105, 107, 108

Reagan, 2, 15
recipient countries, 7, 8, 15, 28, 35
ROK, 102, 103
RSA, 99

SALs, 3, 34
SAP, 2, 29, 33, 37
SDF, 42, 43
SDGs, 39, 42, 45
SECALs, 8
sector investment program, 8
self-help efforts, 15, 28, 35, 37, 41, 45
Senkaku, 92
South–South Cooperation, 49, 70, 79, 84
South Sudan, 3
SSA, 3, 11, 12, 17, 20, 23, 24, 29, 36, 37, 39, 42, 45, 47, 51, 52, 58, 66, 70, 71, 74, 76, 77, 79, 101
State Council, 101, 102, 108, 112
String of Pearls, 109
structural adjustment, 1, 3, 10–12

Tanzania-Zambia railway, 66
Tazara Railway, 47, 67, 68, 109
Thatcher, 2, 15
third-country technical assistance, 18
three-pronged approach, 81

TICAD, 39, 41, 42, 89, 94, 96, 97, 102, 118
Trump, 103, 107, 114

UNCTAD, 50, 54
UNMDGs, 10
  MDGs, 13, 39, 42, 45
United Nations Security Council, 93, 96
USAID, 64, 84

Washington Consensus, 1, 2, 34, 37, 73, 79, 81
Wen, 93, 94, 101, 102
Western countries, 1, 7, 13

white paper, 50, 60, 61, 64–66, 72, 79, 81, 86, 87
World Bank, 2, 3, 5–8, 11–13, 15, 29, 31, 33, 34, 37, 44, 57, 75, 78, 81, 88
World Investment Report, 50
WTO, 48, 50

Xi, 67, 71, 72, 91, 93, 96, 98, 101, 105–110, 112, 114

Yasukuni Shrine, 92, 104, 106, 114

Zaire, 68

Printed in the United States
By Bookmasters